Michigan Opera Theatre

Michigan Opera Theatre

The DiChiera Legacy

Timothy Paul Lentz

For Diana

© 2017 by Timothy Paul Lentz
All rights reserved

ISBN 978-0-692-79493-7

All photos in this book appear by permission of Michigan Opera Theatre
Design and layout by Andrew Katz
Cover image by John Grigaitis

Contents

Foreword by David DiChiera — vii
Foreword by Wayne S. Brown — ix
Acknowledgments — xi

1 The History of Michigan Opera Theatre — 1

2 The Detroit Opera House — 59

3 The Operas — 71
   A Gallery of Selected Images — 74

Appendix 1: MOT Donor Honor Roll — 117
Appendix 2: MOT Dance Productions — 118
Appendix 3: MOT Premieres — 120
Appendix 4: MOT's Community Programs Department Premieres — 122
About the Author — 123

Foreword

In 1991, a young man came into my office and told me he wanted to write a history of Michigan Opera Theatre as his Ph.D. dissertation at Wayne State University. We hit it off right away; it was a happy meeting between someone who wanted to do this project and someone who wanted to see it done. The beginnings of this company go back to the early 1960s, so over the years we had collected a significant amount of programs, newspaper articles, radio and TV interviews, photos, and the like. Of course, none of this material was organized. So when Tim Lentz came into my life, I was excited.

At the time, our arrangement was simple: I would provide full access to all that we had collected, and Tim, as he worked through the materials for his dissertation, would organize it.

Throughout the 1990s, Tim immersed himself in all things Michigan Opera Theatre, becoming a fixture in our offices and actively participating in many of our events and activities; he was an extraordinary addition to the Michigan Opera Theatre family. In fact, in anticipation of the historical grand opening of the Detroit Opera House (1996), Tim had become so engrossed with the company that I asked him to create an overview piece on the history of MOT for both the Gala Opening and the first season in the Opera House.

In the spring of 2001, Tim submitted his dissertation, "The History of Michigan Opera: The Formative Years, 1963–1985," which was unanimously approved. In 2006, when Dr. Lentz retired from the Rochester Community Schools, I was thrilled that he agreed to continue his great work with Michigan Opera Theatre, this time as an employee in a role that he was uniquely qualified to fulfill: archivist / historian / resource library director. The countless hours that went into Tim's dissertation research, coupled with his genuine love for Michigan Opera Theatre, resulted in the Michigan Opera Theatre Library/Archive, which includes a virtual library. Go to www.michiganopera.org and click on "Resource Library" at the bottom of the home page to find a wealth of information about Michigan Opera Theatre.

Now, with this spectacular publication, we benefit once again from Tim's extraordinary passion for our beloved Michigan Opera Theatre. I am grateful beyond words that this wonderful scholar walked into my office twenty-five years ago.

DAVID DICHIERA
Founder and Artistic Director, Michigan Opera Theatre

Foreword

The Michigan Opera Theatre story, with its humble beginnings, meteoric rise, and epic challenges, is one befitting a grand opera. It is a uniquely American story, in which ingredients of passion, determination, and elbow grease result in dreams realized. Of course, what would an opera be without a leading man, who, despite seemingly insurmountable odds, becomes a victorious hero?

Though far from complete, the Michigan Opera Theatre story is ripe to be told, and with the exception of David DiChiera himself, I can think of no individual more qualified, more invested, more enthusiastic to tell it than Dr. Timothy Lentz.

For nearly two decades, Dr. Lentz has served as the MOT archivist and director of the Allesee Resource Library. Through his lens, he has viewed Michigan Opera Theatre from a "front row" vantage point. Now, with *Michigan Opera Theatre*, he shares that view with the reader. From the Overture to Opera years to the historic grand opening of the majestic Detroit Opera House, Dr. Lentz insightfully outlines the rise of an opera company in a city on the brink and its ultimate role as the catalyst for the cultural renaissance of Detroit.

Through eloquently written narrative and splendid photography, the following pages captivatingly guide the reader through the evolution of the Michigan Opera Theatre we know today.

I am exceedingly grateful to Dr. Lentz for the work he has done in providing this extraordinary account. And, of course, I offer my gratitude to David DiChiera, our victorious hero who has effectively championed opera in Detroit. Through his leadership on a national scale, he has been a pioneer for opera in America!

WAYNE S. BROWN
President and CEO, Michigan Opera Theatre

Acknowledgments

There are many people who have helped to bring this book to life. First and foremost, I want to express my profound appreciation for the constant support of David DiChiera. Ever since I arrived on the MOT scene in 1991, he has been an enthusiastic mentor, friend, and source of inspiration. It is his encouraging and positive attitude toward this project that has brought it to life, and for that I am exceedingly grateful.

The photography in this book is of fundamental importance, and special thanks go to two people for their efforts. Bryce Rudder, senior librarian in the Resource Library, has led the way on all the images up to 2005. He has been in charge of the digitization of all the images in the pre-digital-photography era. John Grigaitis, MOT's current, excellent photographer, is in charge of the digital archive of images from 2005 to the present, and his contribution has been formidable. My sincere appreciation goes out to both of these dedicated and talented colleagues.

I would like to express my deep gratitude to Mick Lentz and Armando Delicato as they have been my supporters, counselors, and proof readers from the beginning. Sincere thanks to Andrew Katz for his expertise and professionalism. My colleagues and friends in the MOT family have provided much support, and I wish to thank Karen VanderKloot DiChiera, Wayne Brown, Patricia Walker, Margarite Fourcroy, Bill Austin, Chris Farr, Christy Gray, Mike Hauser, Mitch Carter, Laura Nealssohn, Mark Vondrak, David Osborne, Suzanne Mallare Acton, Elizabeth Anderson, Dan Brinker, Richard Leech, Ken Saltzman, Kim Smith, John Kinsora, Dennis Wells, Johnny Benavides, Suzanne Hanna, Randy Elliott, Tunisia Brown, Shawn Taffinder, Rita Winters, and Rock Monroe.

Special thanks go to my colleagues in the MOT Resource Library: Armando Delicato, Bryce Rudder, Karen Nagher, Larry Glowczewski, Priscila Verani, Elizabeth Zerwekh, and Matt Tansek. Paul Gallagher, Sandy Yee, and Stephen Bajjaly at WSU's School of Library and Information Science have been terrific partners, and thanks to Kathryn Wildfong and Emily Nowak at WSU Press. Also, from the WSU Theatre Department, my sincere appreciation to Blair Anderson, Tony Schmitt, Lavinia Moyer Hart, Ray Ferguson, and Phillip Fox.

I am blessed to have such a wonderful and supportive family. I wish everyone could have loving parents like Rex and Violet Lentz and caring, encouraging brothers and sisters like Mick and Gail Lentz, Rob and Laurie Davis, Liz and Mike Dolan, and Dan G. Carlson. Finally, I would like to express my deepest gratitude for my wife, Diana Lentz. Her constant enthusiasm, graceful nature, unconditional support, strength of character, and loving heart are what sustain me.

1 The History of Michigan Opera Theatre

"Michigan Opera Theatre is a triumph of regional opera. David DiChiera's uncompromising good sense, long-term patience and touch of class have substantiated his idea. His work in Detroit is a model of audience-building technique, his company stands as an example of what opera can mean to Americans." This quote from *Opera News* appeared just a few short years after the establishment of Michigan Opera Theatre (MOT). It was almost inconceivable to all but a handful of people in the 1960s and early 1970s that Detroit could or would support, financially as well as emotionally, its own opera company. Yet Michigan Opera Theatre quickly gained a reputation as one of the nation's fastest-growing and most innovative regional opera companies and, more recently, as one of the country's premier producers of opera and musical theatre.

Building an institution, in this case a world-class opera company, requires a convergence of people and elements as well as a dedicated community, eager to sustain the idea. Michigan Opera Theatre in Detroit, Michigan, is the result of just such a convergence. David DiChiera, the founder of MOT, arrived at the right time in a community that was fertile ground, and indeed, a convergence took place, one that precipitated the building of a major cultural institution and made a major contribution to the renaissance of a city.

In order to trace the very beginnings of MOT, a brief look back at the Detroit Grand Opera Association (DGOA) is in order. It all began in 1943 when the DGOA, a group of influential arts patrons and prominent civic leaders, came forth with a proposal to bring the Philadelphia La Scala Opera Company to Detroit. After eight seasons, the DGOA changed course and brought in the New York City Opera. By the end of the 1957 season, the DGOA, faced with declining attendance, decided that it had to go out and get the best, the prestigious Metropolitan Opera (Met) Tour. Led by grand opera champion Frank Donovan, the longtime leader of efforts to bring grand opera to Detroit, and with the support of Mrs. Anne McDonald Ford, the DGOA presented the first of many years of Met Tours beginning in May 1959.

As chairman of the DGOA Volunteer Committee, Mrs. Ford built a strong organization that included an Education Committee, chaired by Jennie Jones. The Education Committee's purpose was to develop the interest of colleges and school systems and to find a mechanism to distribute lower-priced tickets, while generally promoting the Met Tour. As part of this effort, in 1961, Jones created a small local company of artists, which was called Overture to Opera (OTO), to perform excerpts from the upcoming Met Tour repertory at various locations in metropolitan Detroit. At each OTO performance, a panel would discuss and interpret the scenes that the audience was about to see.

The time was right, the community was ready, and in the fall of 1962, the right person showed up to lead the way, someone who would bring together all the forces. On August 3, Michigan State University Oakland, as it was known in those days, announced the appointment of twelve new staff members. Included in the group was twenty-seven-year-old David DiChiera, and his appointment to the faculty was to be effective August 15, 1962.

David DiChiera

It is important to understand that the names David DiChiera and Michigan Opera Theatre are essentially synonymous in the first era of this opera company. Their history is completely intertwined; they are indeed virtually one and the same. This premise must be introduced in order to honestly and effectively tell the story. It illuminates the idea that to build an opera company, the right person must be found to lead the diverse forces and meld them into a working entity that can achieve the desired goal. In the first era in the company's history, it was DiChiera at the helm: impresario. He has been at the heartbeat from the beginning, involved with every aspect of the company aesthetically and economically, an astute businessman with unparalleled people skills. Even more importantly, he has been the visionary, the guiding spirit. At this writing, it has been almost a fifty-year commitment.

DiChiera was born on April 8, 1935, in McKeesport, Pennsylvania, where his musical sensibilities began quite early. "My love affair with opera began when I was only four, back in McKeesport, Pennsylvania, where I was born. I heard it on the radio and fell head over heels for it," he recalled. DiChiera was the youngest of four children, and his parents, who were immigrant Italians, moved to Los Angeles when he was ten. His father was a laborer, and no one in the family was particularly musical. "Being the youngest gave me certain opportunities, however. None of the others went to college. And when I wanted a piano, my sister saved her money from her job to buy one, and my mother did housework to pay for the lessons." He practiced in the garage of their home every night, and along with the practice, came his first efforts at composition. He began giving recitals at fourteen and played for various clubs and organizations, and while there was never much money involved, it was good experience. He graduated from Canoga Park High School in 1952 as valedictorian and was named all-around outstanding student. In the fall of 1952, he entered UCLA, assisted by a scholarship, and he graduated in 1956 with highest honors, honorary membership in Phi Beta Kappa and a bachelor of arts degree.

UCLA was apparently a very good fit, and DiChiera stayed for his graduate work. He earned his master of arts degree in composition after completion of an original piano concerto. He left for Europe in 1958 after having been awarded a

David DiChiera with Jeffrey H. Foote as Sarastro in *The Magic Flute* in 1977

Fulbright Fellowship for study primarily in Italy. At the time, he was commissioned by the U.S. Information Service to compose a piano sonata for the Naples Festival of Contemporary Italian and American Music. The work was broadcast nationally and highly praised by the Italian press for its "melodic inspiration" and "vivid harmonic color." He continued his studies in musicology and completed his Ph.D. in August 1962.

His tenure at UCLA was summarized by the following letter of recommendation: "David is one of the most brilliant students that we have ever had at UCLA. I am certain that my colleagues here will back me up in this. He is a first rate teacher, pianist, composer, and musicologist. His particular specialties are piano teaching, music history and opera. I feel that he could handle any opera workshop situation with great musical integrity and insight. It is with great pleasure that I highly recommend him to you."

There is indeed a certain cachet, a certain charisma about DiChiera. It was perceived right away and is still firmly in place. DiChiera could just as easily be found at a state senate hearing on the arts in Lansing as attending operatic auditions in New York. Or you could see him at a poolside party in Bloomfield Hills as often as in a community center delivering a lecture or discussing theory with a music student as negotiating a theatrical contract. At the time, *Impresario* magazine described this unique man: "The remarkable part is that in each situation he is perfectly at home, perfectly capable, and (in most instances) perfectly delighted with it all. Once described as a 'suave ramrod,' DiChiera's easy, gracious manner is fortified by an internal discipline that requires him to see all sides of a situation before making decisions and to maintain a schedule that would make physically larger men wilt."

He was always impeccably dressed, charming, knowledgeable, completely comfortable in front of large groups or one to one, and his reputation grew quickly. Simply stated, DiChiera had, and continues to have, the kind of magnetism that is perhaps the key ingredient in the makeup of an impresario. Many years later, Brooks Peters described him succinctly in *Opera News*: "I can see why he's so popular. DiChiera is debonair, with boundless energy and an ability to soothe over-wrought tempers effortlessly." As it turned out, this would indeed be the man around whom the forces would coalesce.

In the fall of 1962, as a young assistant professor at Oakland University, fresh out of the UCLA Music School's doctoral program, DiChiera was a frequent performer and lecturer in the community. Along with his teaching responsibilities, there were many recitals and lectures where the networking began. In fact, it was these lectures, recitals, and performances that led him into the community and the collective that would become MOT. From its very beginnings, MOT was built on the grass-roots efforts of a community-based program. The long-range success of an institution such as MOT depends on broad community-based support where there is a palpable sense of the pride of ownership, both financially and emotionally.

The Overture to Opera Years

David DiChiera was asked to take charge of Overture to Opera in 1963. He caught the attention of Virginia Yntema, who was DGOA general chairman, following Mrs. Ford and Mrs. Lenore Romney in that post. It was Mrs. Yntema who suggested DiChiera for director of Overture to Opera. He was especially effective as a member of the panels that discussed the operas after the performances. His expertise and enthusiastic demeanor in these discussions had created quite a reputation for him in the community, and he was named producer-director for the 1963 season, Overture to Opera III. In its nine seasons, OTO laid the groundwork, established the reputation, secured the financial support, and gained the respectability that allowed for the founding of what was to become Michigan Opera Theatre.

It was during the course of all this activity, in 1963, that DiChiera met and courted Karen VanderKloot, the young woman who would become his bride. "I met Karen at a dinner party at Isabel Himelhoch's. Isabel told me I was going to meet a girl who was very talented musically. Karen played one of her own compositions—she's actually far more original than I am—and the first thing I said was, 'Let me hear that middle section again'—playing teacher right away, you understand. Karen, naturally, thinks, 'Well, just who *is* this guy?' I really must have seemed like an arrogant you-know-what. Fortunately the relationship improved." Indeed it did. If one went to central casting and asked for the perfect spouse, friend, and partner for this young man who would be impresario, they would have sent Karen VanderKloot. Talented, steeped in a deep sense of community

David DiChiera with Ruth Townsend and Virginia Yntema in 1963

involvement, she was the perfect complement to the young assistant professor from California. Many years later, in the dedication that DiChiera wrote for the commemorative program book for the Gala Opening of the Detroit Opera House, he talked about the devotion and support that had sustained him and thanked her publicly, saying, "First and foremost has been Karen VanderKloot DiChiera, for 25 years my companion and forever my most faithful friend, critic and counselor. Her contribution to shaping the first decade of activities at the Music Hall and her impact on having MOT touch the lives of thousands of children and adults throughout the state is incalculable." She had deep roots in the community. It was fortuitous that they would come together and a relationship would bloom. Within a year and a half of that first meeting, they married, on July 20, 1965, in Las Vegas, and formed a lifelong partnership. This was not only a talented young woman but also one who grew up with a legacy of volunteerism and of giving to the community. She was well suited to the role she would take in the venture of building an opera company. Much later, in an interview, she explained, "Early on I began to understand how to get into a community and who to put together with whom, and how to mix it up and how to have fun with it."

The idea of starting an opera company was already percolating. DiChiera was talking about starting an opera company before he was married. Karen recounted, "It was going to be opera, always. Then he became chairman of the Music Department at Oakland. When Woody Varner asked David to do this, he knew that he was getting the Yntemas, the Townsends, so Ford Motor, Chrysler, and GM—my uncle was president of Chevrolet. He had the big three hooked up, so David was

Karen and David DiChiera in the lobby of Music Hall Theatre in 1972

a very powerful chairperson of the Music Department." DiChiera had come to Oakland University because the university itself was new, and he saw a wonderful opportunity to create and build programs. During the middle 1960s, besides directing Overture to Opera, he was instrumental in starting the university's major cultural programs, the Meadow Brook Festival and Meadow Brook Theatre, but it was the building of an opera company that was to hold his primary interest.

DiChiera's first three seasons with OTO were, as planned, programs of scenes from the operas to be performed by the Met in its annual Detroit season. Typically, DiChiera would introduce the opera to the audience and fill them in on relevant opera and music history. It was very much like what Leonard Bernstein was so good at, and popular for, when he addressed the audience in his famous Young People's Concerts. DiChiera was very comfortable in this format; he was very well received by the audiences, and the OTO seasons became very popular.

The DGOA had always thought of the OTO program as its educational arm and a promotional vehicle for the Met Tour. DiChiera, however, saw it as a chance to develop something local that belonged to the city. In a 1982 article in the *Ann Arbor News*, he reflected, "Detroit was the fifth largest city in the nation and the only major city without an opera company. I couldn't accept that fact; I knew the constituency for it was here." He was committed to the idea that the future of opera in America was the continued growth of regional opera.

DiChiera was determined to make a difference, and for the 1964 season of Overture to Opera III, he doubled the number of performances from the previous year to twelve, which included three matinees for students. They took place all over the Detroit metropolitan area, from Bloomfield Hills to Hamtramck, from Detroit to Trenton. Each location had volunteers in place as ticket chairpersons. The most extensive education program ever undertaken by the DGOA, it featured four scenes: *Aida*, act 2, scene 1; *Don Giovanni*, act 1, scenes 2 and 3; *La Bohème*, act 1, scene 2; and the final scene from *Faust*. The program was jointly sponsored by the DGOA, Oakland University, University Center for Adult Education (a joint effort by Eastern Michigan University, Wayne State University, and University of Michigan), and the Detroit Public Library.

DiChiera assembled what can be considered stellar local casts and production teams, and looking back now, one is struck by the assemblage of names during the OTO years. It is a veritable who's who of Detroit-area talent. Two interchangeable casts were used. Interchangeable casts would become the standard procedure for OTO. It provided more opportunities for singers, and of course, backups were always available and ready in case of emergency.

Rodney Stenborg as Don Giovanni and Doralene McNelly as Donna Elvira from *Don Giovanni* in 1964

1966

In 1966, an article in the Met Tour program on OTO made special note regarding Barbara Gibson, playing the "Mad Scene" in *Lucia di Lammermoor*: it marked the return of Barbara Gibson to the opera stage after an absence of eight years. Appearing many times on television and radio with Toscanini, Miss Gibson made her professional debut on the *Bell Telephone Hour*. Gibson would become Mrs. Sam B. Williams and a leading supporter of MOT. She served on the MOT board for most of its history and made several key contributions during the formative years.

DiChiera expanded the original format of Overture to Opera in 1967. It had grown and for the first time included a complete work, the Michigan premiere of Cherubini's one-act opera *The Portuguese Inn*. Collins George of the *Detroit Free Press* expressed the public's growing enthusiasm in the 1967 OTO program: "The verve, the spirit with which everything is presented, the way the company can capture and project a dramatic movement; in general, the high level of competence of the performances make them worthwhile.... The real lesson of the Overture company is that there is a place in Detroit for an operatic stock company.... Thanks must be expressed to DiChiera for this awakening to awareness of opera of such a large segment of the population."

DiChiera was quoted in the 1967 Met Tour program on two key areas. First, he continued to articulate and further establish his philosophy that opera should be

Edward Kingins and Alice Dutcher in a scene from *Samson and Delilah* in 1965

8   The History of Michigan Opera Theatre

John Broome as Toby and Emily Derr as Monica from *The Medium* in 1967

vital theatre. For this reason, the productions were sung in English, which gave the audience a real contact with the drama and a clearer insight into the relationship between words and music. He spoke on a second subject that was another of the primary themes during the formative years, which was the potential for the revitalization of opera in the Detroit area. "If we nurture our own talent, and give them a chance to develop their skills right here, then we can look forward to an exciting development in Detroit musical life."

The progress and growth continued in the 1968 OTO season, which featured Gian Carlo Menotti's *The Medium*, a tragedy, along with a revival of the comic one-act opera *The Portuguese Inn*. The highlights of the season were two performances where the world-famous Muriel Greenspon sang the lead role in *The Medium*. These were historical mileposts in that they were OTO's first performances with an orchestra, on March 26 and 27, 1968. The orchestra was made up of members of the Detroit Symphony Orchestra and was conducted by longtime OTO colleague William C. Byrd. Overall, there were six evening performances and fifteen student matinees that were seen by over fifteen thousand students.

Right: Peter Bicklemann as The Teacher, James Adams as The Boy, and cast from *Der Jasager* in 1969

Below, top: Judy Johnston as Serafina and Robert Denison as Don Annibale Pistacchio in a scene from *Il Campanello* in 1969

Below, bottom: J. B. Davis as Dr. Bartolo, Maria Ewing as Rosina, and Thomas Palmer as Figaro from *The Barber of Seville* in 1970

1969

Adventurous programming marked the 1969 season, which featured two short complete works, both Michigan premieres: Kurt Weill's grimly striking *Der Jasager* and the wonderfully comic *Il Campanello* by Donizetti. The season was enhanced by the appearance of the operatic star Italo Tajo, as the frustrated bridegroom in *Il Campanello*. Tajo was an internationally recognized figure in the opera world. At the time, Tajo was artist-in-residence and director of the opera workshop at the University of Cincinnati's Conservatory of Music. He was introduced to DiChiera by Barbara Gibson Williams, who had sung Rosina to his Don Basilio in *The Barber of Seville* for the San Francisco Opera in 1953. Tajo had performed in opera houses all over the world, including La Scala, three seasons with the Metropolitan, and nine with the San Francisco Opera. He was the first recognized, world-class artist employed by OTO, and his performance at the Detroit Institute of Arts (DIA) on February 28, 1969, was a most notable occasion. The *Detroit Free Press* sounded what had become a familiar theme: "The real moral of the evening, however, is what it has been for several years. If a night of such operatic professionalism can be achieved by local talent in Detroit, why can't there be a completely successful opera company here?"

The next step for OTO was the crowning achievement of the first decade. For the 1970 season, OTO produced its first full-length opera, Rossini's comic masterpiece *The Barber of Seville*, starring then nineteen-year-old Detroiter Maria Ewing in her professional debut. Italo Tajo was back, this time as stage director, and William Byrd was once again music director. There were nine performances, four of which were student matinees. In an important development, one performance, on April 8 at the DIA, was with full orchestra instead of just piano accompaniment. The season closed with an April 21 performance in Midland, Michigan, sponsored by the Northwood Institute.

This was clearly a formidable group, and they collected a very positive series of reviews. The *Free Press* called the DIA performance with orchestra "completely

10   The History of Michigan Opera Theatre

successful" and stated, "By now one has come to expect fine entertainment from these Overtures and is never disappointed." The real success of the evening, however, must be traced to Italo Tajo. The *Free Press* continued, "Not only was there never a static moment in the production but each person was thoroughly trained in even the tiniest bits of stage business. The sets were ingenuously simple. The small pit orchestra was conducted on a high level by William Byrd, of Flint." The *Detroit News* stated, "Musically, it was a buoyant, graceful, attractive production with fresh, young and agile principal voices, neatly dovetailed ensemble work and close coordination between the pit and stage." Overture to Opera was becoming a full-fledged opera company, one in search of a home.

The Music Hall Years

Overture to Opera ended its ten nomadic years in 1971 with its first season in the Music Hall, which included productions of Andrew Lloyd Weber's *Joseph and the Amazing Technicolor Dreamcoat* and Puccini's *La Rondine* (both were Michigan premieres). The opera company as we know it today had its inception in the fall of 1971 with the company's move into the Music Hall Theatre. Overture to Opera had laid the groundwork: a committee that would become MOT's first Board of Trustees had been formed, and with the move into the Music Hall, there was now a home base from which to work. In addition, as a major contribution to the

Nancy Shade as Magda from *La Rondine* in 1971

David Patrick Kelly as Joseph and cast from *Joseph and the Amazing Technicolor Dream Coat* in 1971

The History of Michigan Opera Theatre   11

quality of life in southeast Michigan, let history show that the company's move into the Music Hall, saving it from the wrecking ball, was the spark that ignited the rebirth of Detroit's now magnificent theatre and entertainment district. David DiChiera and his young opera company were the first to commit to downtown and reinvest in a district that had seen many years of serious decline. It was a most significant moment in the history of Detroit.

Ruth and Lynn Townsend

The 1971 season program was the first OTO program that listed an Overture to Opera Committee. This group of dedicated individuals, led by committee cochairmen Lynn and Ruth Townsend, soon became the Founding Members of the Board of Directors of Michigan Opera Theatre. Also listed was a much larger group of people, organizations, and corporations called the Friends of Overture to Opera. These groups had been formed separately from the DGOA as entities of their own. The financial and personal contributions of these prestigious groups provided the foundation that allowed for the inception of MOT. Mr. and Mrs. Townsend led the way with a love of opera and a deep, genuine sense of commitment. DiChiera recalled, "The evolution of Michigan Opera Theatre found refuge under the dedicated leadership of Ruth and Lynn Townsend, who brought together a group of founding members to provide financial support and loving care for a fragile and young enterprise. It was Lynn whose considerable influence as chairman of the board of the Chrysler Corporation opened the doors in the community to pay attention to what he affectionately called 'David's Project.' He oversaw the transition from Overture to Opera as a touring program of scenes

David DiChiera with Ruth and Lynn Townsend

to the establishment of an opera company and the saving of Music Hall as its first home."

Ruth Townsend served as chairman of the Overture to Opera Committee from the very beginning in 1963, when DiChiera took the reins of the educational initiative of the DGOA. She organized an extensive network of volunteers representing each of the communities where the performances of Overture to Opera took place. Her early leadership was nurtured further by her husband, Lynn, who possessed a profound interest and love for the genre of opera. Together with their committee volunteers, Mr. and Mrs. Townsend dedicated themselves to the success of Overture to Opera. Through their determination, they inspired much of the organizational framework that ensured the growth of Overture's programs and helped galvanize the community's greater interest in establishing a full-time, professional opera company in Detroit.

1972

In 1972, DiChiera's company, still formally known as the Detroit Grand Opera Association's Overture to Opera Company, was officially accepted as a member of OPERA America, the national association of professional opera companies. DiChiera's dedicated involvement in OPERA America over the years has put Michigan Opera Theatre in the mainstream of the opera world. During his two terms as president in the 1980s, the organization more then doubled in size. DiChiera was in the middle of the action as the organization galvanized the philosophies and practices that have defined its existence. His association with OPERA America over the years clearly shows David DiChiera as a major presence and key leader in the regional opera company movement in the United States in the last quarter of the twentieth century.

Phyllis Curtin as Floria Tosca from *Tosca* in 1972

The company presented yet another eclectic mainstage season in 1972, which included Puccini's *Tosca*, featuring the internationally recognized soprano Phyllis Curtin in the tile role. Also featured was a revival of Menotti's *The Medium*, for which DiChiera brought back Muriel Greenspon to sing the title role and contracted film star Sal Mineo to direct and play the role of the deaf-mute Toby. DiChiera had been looking for someone with some star power, and the announcement of Sal Mineo's involvement created a terrific buzz in the media.

DiChiera is a genius at this sort of casting and programming, tapping into the star community to enhance the prestige and the public-relations potential of the company's activities. Time and again throughout the company's history, usually with impeccable timing to maximize the positive impact, DiChiera has contracted someone or some event with genuine star power. The popular excitement that this creates, the boost to the marketing and public-relations departments, and the prestige it gives the company are all important results. It is a critically important trait for an impresario. Marc Scorca, the president and CEO of OPERA America, was quoted in 2001, "David is as savvy a producer as there is in our business.

Sal Mineo as Toby and Muriel Greenspon as Madame Flora from *The Medium* in 1972

He has tremendous insight into the sensibility of his audience, his community and what he can do in terms of interesting programming and what he must do to pay the bills."

The 1972 season continued the company's extensive education and outreach activities. This was the year the company created the Opera in Residence program, in which Michigan communities were able to host the OTO Company in their town for a week of opera experience. The week would include classes, workshops, and a full production featuring members of the community and MOT professionals. The outreach and education aspect of the organization, under the inspired and dedicated leadership of Karen VanderKloot DiChiera, was to continue to be a key factor in the building and solidifying of an audience for this regional opera company. The Community Programs Department over the years made an invaluable contribution to the character and the strength of the company and has earned national recognition for its varied and unique programming.

The Music Hall years began with a clear goal, to establish a permanent, full-time professional opera company in Detroit. In order to put this into context, it must be understood that the goal almost immediately became twofold: first to establish an opera company and second to contribute to the renaissance of the city of Detroit. What evolved at the Music Hall was not one but two major arts institutions: a professional opera company and a performing arts center. What evolved in the larger sense was a world-class theatre and entertainment district.

There was indeed a larger cultural picture. It was a unique and very difficult time in the history of Detroit. The riots in 1967 had torn the city apart. The flight

14   The History of Michigan Opera Theatre

to the suburbs was in full swing, and many people considered Detroit a war zone. What had once been a vital and thriving theatre district was almost completely dormant.

DiChiera and his committee were fully cognizant of the times and the challenges facing the city, and they welcomed the opportunity to make a difference. They were poised to contribute in a way that would help establish a positive identity for the city. It was at this time that the idea of a renaissance in the city was starting to grow and take hold. The Renaissance Center had its ground-breaking in 1972. DiChiera and his forces were at the center of it all, and he enjoyed the dynamics that were evolving at the Music Hall because he was also "dealing with the large problems of a city. The civic, political, and cultural aspects of a city have to work together. There's a tremendous thrill in that too." This twofold goal

David DiChiera in front of the Music Hall in 1972

of establishing a professional regional opera company and contributing to the rebirth of the city reflects the cultural impact of Michigan Opera Theatre's leading position in Detroit's reborn theatre district and continues right up to the present day at the Detroit Opera House.

In March 1973, the company officially changed its name to Michigan Opera Theatre. The time had come for the company to formally establish its own identity and begin the process of separating from the Detroit Grand Opera Association. Michigan Opera Theatre—the name was a natural. It evolved out of DiChiera's philosophies of serving the entire state and of presenting a full range of opera and music theatre. DiChiera felt that the future of opera in America was with regional opera companies. He set in motion several philosophies that would provide a foundation for the future, the first of which was to establish broad grassroots, community-based support. He felt it was critical to produce opera as vital theatre, and in English, to make it accessible and theatrically immediate. It was also critical to continually strive for artistic integrity by featuring the finest professional work. This would require a dedication to adventurous and diverse programming covering the full range of opera and music theatre. Furthermore, an eclectic, hands-on, humanities approach to education, outreach, and community programs would be crucial. DiChiera also believed that he needed to establish and nurture a firm commitment to dance and address the need to develop a concept of arts advocacy.

Citizen Initiative Working through Private Enterprise

It was at this time, in the spring of 1973, that the Overture to Opera Committee became the Founding Members of the Board of Directors of Michigan Opera Theatre. The importance of the committed effort by this dedicated group of supporters cannot be overstated. Their foresight and support made the dream possible. They are the following:

Mr. and Mrs. Lynn A. Townsend, Founding Chairmen
Mr. and Mrs. Avern L. Cohn
Mr. and Mrs. John DeCarlo
Dr. and Mrs. David DiChiera
Mr. and Mrs. Aaron H. Gershenson
Mr. and Mrs. Donald C. Graves
Honorable and Mrs. Roman S. Gribbs
Mr. and Mrs. John C. Griffin
Mr. and Mrs. Harry L. Jones
Honorable and Mrs. Wade McCree Jr.
Mr. Harry J. Nederlander
Mr. E. Harwood Rydholm
Mr. and Mrs. Neil Snow

Mr. and Mrs. Richard Stirchartz
Mr. and Mrs. Robert C. VanderKloot
Mr. and Mrs. Sam B. Williams
Mr. and Mrs. Theodore O. Yntema

To make it all work, to establish in people that palpable sense of the pride of ownership, both emotionally and financially, there had to be a dedicated and devoted leader. That was David DiChiera. From the very beginning he immersed himself in the community and created an excitement on which he could build an opera company. It was a labor of love, and it was combined with an intense, full-time, every-single-day kind of effort that would inspire the forces around him to coalesce into Michigan Opera Theatre.

Music Hall Center for the Performing Arts

Though the opera company had finally found a comfortable home in Music Hall, the building's future was by no means secure. To save it from the wrecking ball, a group of citizens came together and established the not-for-profit Music Hall Center for the Performing Arts. In May 1973, DiChiera was selected as the first executive director of the Music Hall Center. As such, he would be wearing two hats, general director of Michigan Opera Theatre and executive director of the new Music Hall Center for the Performing Arts. He ran MOT from offices on one floor of the Music Hall and the Performing Arts Center from separate offices on a different floor. Wearing two hats for the first of many times agreed with DiChiera as well as both organizations.

MOT marked its third season by bringing major productions to Kalamazoo and Flint in 1973. These performances, along with MOT's expanding Opera in Residence program, which visited nine different communities, showed MOT expanding its base, building its audience, and tending to its mission to serve as the operatic resource for the entire state. This is also the year of MOT's first venture into the realm of light opera at the Music Hall, with Lehar's *The Merry Widow*, and its most mammoth production to date, Mussorgsky's masterpiece *Boris Godunov* in its seldom-heard original version, starring the world-famous bass Jerome Hines in the title role.

The incredible and varied programming at the Music Hall Center also continued and was filling a major void in the cultural life of the Detroit metropolitan area and beyond. The company's continuing tour of communities, from Livonia to Traverse City, established MOT as one of Michigan's major cultural resources. Thousands of Michigan residents had the opportunity to enjoy opera as the touring company presented workshops, seminars, and productions in classrooms, gymnasiums, and theatres throughout the state. At the Music Hall, the mainstage season was highlighted by MOT's first production of Donizetti's *The Elixir of Love* as well as MOT's first production of George Gershwin's beloved *Porgy and Bess*,

Jerome Hines as Boris Godunov from *Boris Godunov* in 1974

David DiChiera with Leona Mitchell in front of the Music Hall in 1975

directed by Ella Gerber, known the world over for her association with the powerful folk opera. The production featured a twenty-four-year-old Leona Mitchell, as Bess, at the beginning of a meteoric rise to international stardom.

The debut season at the Music Hall Center for the Performing Arts was by all accounts a tremendous success, and the enthusiastic support in the community was positive and growing. It was an astonishing slate of activities. Suddenly, the people of the Detroit metropolitan area had a single facility they could look to for jazz and popular music, ballet companies, modern dance, theatre, and opera. A vacuum was being filled, and productions and performers whose nationwide tours had skipped Detroit for years now found themselves booked into this great theatre, playing for supportive and appreciative audiences. In a letter to DiChiera dated October 3, 1973, Detroit's Mayor Roman Gribbs summarized the sentiment: "I want to express to you my deep interest and support for what you are doing for

Detroit in your Music Hall venture. It is a much-needed addition to our downtown night life and it provides a fine example of citizen initiative working through private enterprise. I hope you will extend my sincere congratulations and best wishes for success to all those who are working with you on this vital community project." DiChiera and Michigan Opera Theatre were at the center of what was, for the first time in many years, a growing interest and excitement in downtown activities.

A Triumph of Regional Opera

In May 1976, the entertainment journal *Variety* stated, "The flourishing of Michigan Opera Theatre and Music Hall Center for the Performing Arts are due to the efforts of a great many interested people but no one doubts that the prime mover in what is happening in Detroit is 39-year-old David DiChiera. Because of DiChiera, Detroiters now have a spread of theater, music, dance, opera, pop and ethnic entertainment. DiChiera is doing what, three years ago, was thought impossible—he is bringing Detroiters back downtown at night, in droves, and he is garnering a portfolio of excellent reviews."

The Music Hall years were filled with artistic successes, for which MOT quickly established a reputation as an innovative and exciting new company. MOT was thrust into the national limelight in 1976 when it commissioned and produced the world premiere of Thomas Pasatieri's *Washington Square*, starring Catherine Malfitano. An article in *Time* magazine in 1976 stated, "Nothing testifies to the growing up of a regional American opera company quite like a world premiere." The

Chairman Lynn Townsend and Dr. David DiChiera receiving a plaque from Mayor Coleman Young in honor of Michigan Opera Theatre Day in 1974

David DiChiera with Catherine Malfitano, seated at his right, and the cast of *Washington Square* in 1976

Christian Science Monitor dubbed MOT "Detroit's Showcase" and stated in reference to Dr. DiChiera, "He has overcome Detroit's inferiority complex about the arts by mounting events of national interest." *Washington Square* was clearly one of the most important historical mileposts in the company's formative years. *Variety* declared, "This premiere is a first for Michigan Opera Theatre and a milestone for Detroit and Michigan." *Opera News* praised MOT as "a triumph of regional opera."

Other highlights of the company's mainstage Music Hall performances include the professional operatic debut of Kathleen Battle; the revival, telecast, and ensuing Broadway run of *The Most Happy Fella*; the directoral debut of the actor Sal Mineo with *The Medium*, in which he also played Toby; a performance and a national public TV telecast of Aaron Copland's *The Tender Land* with the composer himself on the podium; the American opera debut of Cleo Laine in *The Merry Widow*; and Catherine Malfitano's first *La Traviata*. MOT was one of the first companies to present major premieres of national operas reflecting the makeup of the community it serves: the Polish opera *The Haunted Castle* and the Armenian opera *Anoush*. Further national recognition came from mounting important revivals of such American works as Gershwin's *Porgy and Bess*, Marc Blitzstein's *Regina*, Scott Joplin's *Treemonisha*, and Louis Gruenberg's *The Emperor Jones*. In fact, fully 25 percent of the company's mainstage productions were devoted to opera and musical theater works by American composers.

Left, top: Choreographer Eugene Loring, David DiChiera, and composer Aaron Copland and in rehearsal for the production of *The Tender Land* in 1979

Left, bottom: Carmen Balthrop as Treemonisha and ensemble from *Treemonisha* in 1982

Below: Andrew Smith as Brutus Jones and Daniel Boggess as Henry Smithers from *The Emperor Jones* in 1979

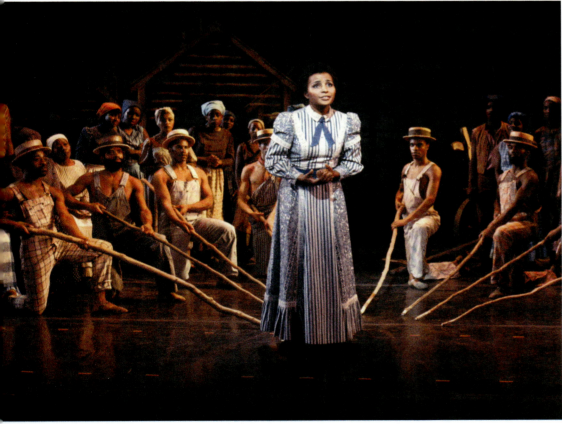

The History of Michigan Opera Theatre

Karen VanderKloot DiChiera

Michigan Opera Theatre's Community Programs Department was founded in 1978 by the nationally prominent composer and arts educator Karen VanderKloot DiChiera. The department's myriad activities included the highly successful Opera in Residence program and all of the company's touring and educational/outreach activities. Karen's diverse, eclectic background, along with her creative, hands-on inclinations, combined with her nationally recognized stature as an educator and composer to make her the perfect choice to lead the department. Throughout her tenure as a full-time volunteer in the early years, involved with every aspect of the company and its formation, she made a contribution to the formative years that is simply incalculable. Now as director of community programs, she would provide the inspired and dedicated leadership that would make her department one of the primary strengths of the company while receiving state and national recognition for its varied and unique programming.

Traveling throughout both peninsulas of Michigan, Karen taught adults and children in classrooms and workshops to create original works through improvisation in music, drama, and dance, bringing these programs to thousands of people. She worked with learning-disabled and emotionally impaired students, directed interpreters to use American sign language for the deaf during performances of MOT, and has created programs for the Oakland County Schools to expose deaf children to music. In 1990, she won the prestigious Governor's Arts in Education Award. Upon her retirement, David DiChiera explained, "It's the individual lives that Karen has touched over the years. That's really the legacy that she has left. The

Karen VanderKloot DiChiera, MOT director of Community Programs

Karen DiChiera teaching in Ludington, Michigan, in 1977

Karen DiChiera teaching in Detroit in 1978

Leona Mitchell as Margeurite and Stephen Dickson as Valentin from *Faust* in 1978

programs are all great, but it's the young people who she has devoted herself to and whose lives have become something that they would never have been—for me that's the Karen story."

This was the year of another truly momentous development, as 1978 also marked the debut of the MOT Orchestra. David DiChiera's longtime colleague and friend Mark Flint was on the podium to conduct the orchestra's first two productions, Bizet's *The Pearl Fishers* and the company's first mainstage production of an American musical, Kern and Hammerstein's *Show Boat*. Another highlight that year was a production of Gounod's *Faust* featuring Leona Mitchell that the *Detroit Free Press* called "heavenly" and the *Eccentric* called "brilliant." DiChiera was named a "Michiganian of the Year" by the *Detroit News* in 1979 and was elected president of OPERA America, the national service organization to which all major professional opera companies belong, a post he held for four years.

In the late 1970s and early 1980s, MOT was evolving as one of America's important cultural forces, reaching an audience of over one hundred thousand annually.

The History of Michigan Opera Theatre 23

The goal of presenting a broad range of repertory was achieved with wonderfully diverse programming, which included an ambitious staging of Tchaikovsky's *Joan of Arc* starring Mignon Dunn as Joan, *Porgy and Bess* featuring Wilhelmenia Fernandez, and Gilbert and Sullivan's *The Mikado* featuring an MOT favorite, Mary Callaghan Lynch. Continuing the exploration of unique nationalistic operas, MOT presented the American premiere of the Polish opera *The Haunted Castle* by Stanislaw Moniuszko, which created a huge outpouring of support from the area's Polish community.

Robert E. Dewar

Robert and Nancy Dewar truly loved opera, and Robert joined the Michigan Opera Theatre Board of Trustees in 1973, two years after the company was founded. Mr. Dewar joined the Board of Directors in 1975. In 1980, when Lynn Townsend stepped down, there was no doubt in anyone's mind that Robert Dewar was the logical successor. His love for opera, together with his stature in the community as chairman of the board of Kmart and his community-wide esteem as a man of integrity and commitment, made him the natural choice.

David DiChiera talked about Mr. Dewar's contribution in his program dedication from the Gala Opening of the Detroit Opera House in 1996. "How lucky we were that Bob was in the wings ready to take up the mantle and how lucky I have been—blessed by the continuity of his leadership and unswerving loyalty to the vision of an opera company with no parameters to its potential as a cultural force. For the past 20 years Robert Dewar has provided the stability and affection for MOT, which has allowed this institution to realize its potential. The dream of an opera house was encouraged by Bob and by a Board of Directors and Trustees who have always functioned as a loving family devoted to the art form and to the community. His leadership provided the strategic planning, the willingness to take risks and ultimately the commitment to a project that many believed was impractical and foolish and impossible. All of us working to achieve this dream were given courage and strength of steadfastness by our community leader and volunteer par excellence, Robert Dewar."

Robert Dewar's passion for the opera permeated his life and activities. Not only was he a generous benefactor, but his commitment took him above and beyond what most people would consider doing. David DiChiera recalls those years leading up to the opening of the Detroit Opera House: "Bob gave of himself tirelessly, and during those years of frantic fund-raising, the Detroit Athletic Club became his second office. I can't count the breakfasts and luncheons that preceded a tour with prospective and incredulous 'prospects.' In the dead of winter or in the blistering summer heat, he would don his hard hat and sell the vision of a beautiful opera house, while walking through a building in complete shambles." Mr. Dewar's commitment was so great that, when the construction teams threatened

Mignon Dunn as Joan from *Joan of Arc* in 1979

24 The History of Michigan Opera Theatre

David DiChiera with Robert and Nancy Dewar

to walk out because the mortgage had not been approved, he put his own finances on the line—the bank trusted him, and his actions allowed the opera house to open in time for its sold-out gala.

Planning for the Future

MOT completed its long-range plan and established its mission to be one of the outstanding opera companies in the United States, serving as a major cultural resource. To achieve this, five goals were established. The first was to present the broadest possible range of music theatre repertoire with the highest artistic standards. The second was to assure that MOT made its work accessible to all segments of the population in a variety of ways. The third goal was to provide opportunities for emerging talent, both local and national. The fourth was a commitment to American works, and the fifth was to develop broad-based financial stability.

In 1981, Suzanne Mallare Acton came to MOT. She began as music director for the Community Programs Department and coach/accompanist for mainstage productions. During that first year, she was also appointed chorus master. This versatile musician has served in every position in the music department, playing the rehearsals, conducting rehearsals when the conductor was out of town, coaching all the singers, chorus master, director of intern programs, assistant conductor, music director of the touring company, and conductor. "Suzanne is a wonderful talent, impeccably musical," said Dr. DiChiera. "She is a taskmaster but in such a way that they respond and admire her greatly. She has managed to inspire an extremely high level of loyalty and commitment." In 1986, her title became

Suzanne Mallare Acton conducting *Too Hot to Handel* in 2008

David Cryer as Sweeney Todd and Judy Kaye as Mrs. Lovett from *Sweeney Todd* in 1984

Dame Joan Sutherland as Anna Bolena from *Anna Bolena* in 1984

assistant music director and chorus master, and she has frequently conducted mainstage productions. She is also director of the MOT Children's Chorus. After more than thirty years of dedicated service, she continues at the heartbeat of MOT's music department.

MOT's final production at the Music Hall was the unique music theatre piece *Sweeney Todd*. It was adventurous programming at its finest, as Dr. DiChiera brought yet another major American work for its Detroit premiere. *Sweeney Todd* closed on December 1, 1984, and when the final curtain came down, the Music Hall years ended in a blaze of glory on the wings of a critically acclaimed aesthetic tour de force. It was a fitting way to end an era.

In 1983, after extensive strategic planning and in anticipation of the imminent demise of the Met Tour, MOT announced its decision to broaden the scope of the company by producing large-scale grand opera at the Masonic Temple Theatre along with the offerings at the Music Hall. The intention was that MOT would begin to take over the Met's role by producing grand opera on the same scale. In 1984, following the Met's spring tour, MOT produced its first grand opera at the Masonic Temple, Bellini's *Anna Bolena*. It featured a cast of international stars including Dame Joan Sutherland and Ben Heppner, conducted by maestro Richard Bonynge, and featuring the Midwest premiere of English surtitles.

In 1985, the DGOA announced that after that May, it would no longer bring the Met to Detroit. The tour had fallen on hard times both artistically and financially. Equally important, the growth of regional companies in host cities like Detroit had made the tour redundant. Once the Metropolitan Opera Tours came to an end, MOT was ready to fill the void. In the spring of 1985, MOT returned to the Masonic Temple for Verdi's *Aida*, starring Leona Mitchell in her first performance in the title role, followed by the Bulgarian soprano Ghena Dimitrova in Puccini's *Turandot* in 1986. These productions marked the beginning of a new era for MOT.

The Masonic Temple / Fisher Theatre Years

MOT celebrated its fifteenth anniversary season in 1985 by moving to the Fisher Theatre for its fall presentations. The administrative offices also moved to the New Center Area. The decision to leave the Music Hall was a difficult one, but ultimately it was a natural evolution considering the momentous growth and impressive goals laid out for the company by DiChiera and the Board of Directors. The vastly different stages of the twenty-one-hundred-seat Fisher Theatre and the four-thousand-seat Masonic Temple (home to the Met Tours for so many years) allowed the company to expand ticket sales and income potential, as well as to express the rich diversity and the quality of its programming.

In January 1985, DiChiera was named general director of Opera Pacific in California's Orange County, which held its first performance season that year on the stage of the new Orange County Performing Arts Center. Now, as general director of the two companies and artistic director of Dayton Opera (a position he held from 1981 to 1991), he could essentially collaborate with himself, sharing the combined artistic resources and leveraging the financial resources of all three institutions for considerable savings and higher-quality productions. This unique tricompany framework that DiChiera headed was regarded as a positive and innovative formula for the future of opera production. DiChiera was indeed on the

James Dietsch as Amonasro and Leona Mitchell as Aida and cast from *Aida* in 1985

Ghena Dimitrova as Princess Turandot from *Turandot* in 1986

The History of Michigan Opera Theatre · 27

David DiChiera in front of the Fisher Theatre in 1985

David DiChiera in front of the Orange County Performing Arts Center

vanguard of the activity in the regional opera company movement in the last quarter of the twentieth century.

In 1985, MOT mounted the first American opera production of Bernstein's *West Side Story*, which enjoyed an extended run. In the 1986–1987 season, MOT increased its mainstage offerings to six productions, mounted its first full grand opera season at the Masonic Temple, and earned its rank as one of the top-ten opera companies in the United States, based on operating budget.

During the 1987–1988 season, with the budget topping $5 million and subscribers numbering over nine thousand, MOT launched its biggest season ever, highlighted by the historic Detroit concert debut of Luciano Pavarotti at a sold-out Joe Louis Arena. Mainstage activity included *Il Trovatore* starring Leona Mitchell, *Die Fledermaus* featuring Jo Anne Worley as Prince Orlofsky, *La Bohème* featuring Stephanie Friede and Marianna Christos, Stephen Sondheim's *Follies* starring Nancy Dussault, Edie Adams, Juliet Prose, and MOT favorite Ron Raines, and *The Pirates of Penzance* starring Gary Sandy and MOT stalwart Mary Callaghan Lynch. The company was proud to also feature the long-awaited return of one of the great American operatic dramas, Douglas Moore's *The Ballad of Baby Doe*. The season opened with MOT's five hundredth public performance and concluded as the sixth consecutive "in the black," financially sound season.

MOT commissioned a new production of Bellini's *Norma* in 1989 from the English artist John Pascoe for Dame Joan Sutherland's final performances of the role. The production earned the company its first NPR broadcast. The same season, MOT added classical ballet to its programming mix with a production of

Swan Lake starring Cynthia Gregory. MOT audiences for mainstage and outreach programs combined exceeded 230,000. The twenty-year-old MOT mounted an acclaimed revival of *Show Boat* in 1990, produced its first-ever Richard Strauss opera, *Ariadne auf Naxos*, starring the sensational Alessandra Marc, and unveiled a new production, designed and directed by John Pascoe, of *Don Giovanni*, which was, like *Norma*, shared by Opera Pacific and Dayton Opera.

Left: David and Karen DiChiera with Luciano Pavarotti at the 1988 Opera Ball

Below, right: Dame Joan Sutherland as Norma from *Norma* in 1989

Below, left: Consuelo Hill as Queenie and ensemble from *Show Boat* in 1990

The History of Michigan Opera Theatre   29

The Search for a New Home

While the move to the Fisher and Masonic Temple theatres achieved a temporary solution to the company's need for greater technical resources, seating capacity, and audience amenities, the strategic planning process begun by DiChiera and the board in the mid-1980s made it clear that the future of the opera company as a permanent resource for the city and state would necessitate a more lasting solution. The opera company had to find or create, and control, a world-class facility to accommodate all of its activities.

In the late 1980s, the company seriously considered renovating the State Theatre next to the newly renovated Fox Theatre, though the arrangement was not considered ideal because the facility was not for sale, only for rent. While in the midst of these discussions, the Grand Circus Theatre became available for purchase. DiChiera considered the magnificent structure ideal because of its opera-house-style interior and the possibilities for building a new stage house. It was after all, a building designed by the legendary theatre architect C. Howard Crane. DiChiera brought in facilities experts to substantiate its structural soundness, acoustical excellence, and technical capabilities when updated. In 1989, the board secured the first parcel in the Grand Circus Theatre block as the company's future performance site.

Philip E. Benton Jr., then president of Ford Motor Company, agreed to chair the Opera House Capital Campaign in 1990. Under his leadership, MOT ran a successful campaign to name the private grand tier boxes, enabling the company to acquire the remaining parcels of the Grand Circus Theatre block by 1994. In the

David DiChiera with Richard Bonynge, Dame Joan Sutherland, and Philip E. Benton Jr. in 1989

30 The History of Michigan Opera Theatre

David DiChiera in front of the old Grand Circus Theatre prior to the Detroit Opera House renovation

Andrii Shkurha as King Roger from *King Roger* in 1991

fall of 1991, during a press conference prior to Luciano Pavarotti's return concert engagement in Detroit, the legendary opera star made the startling promise to return and perform to help open the Detroit Opera House, bringing the project to the attention of the public at large and providing a tremendous boost to the opera house campaign.

Michigan Opera Theatre, with a budget of $5.4 million, had quickly ascended the ranks of its more than one hundred peer companies to assume the prestigious position as one of the top-ten opera companies in the United States. In 1992, MOT was cited by the Ford Foundation as one of the most fiscally responsible arts organizations in the country. Along with *Lucia di Lammermoor*, *Side by Side by Sondheim*, *The Music Man*, and a sumptuous *Sampson and Delilah*, the highlight of the mainstage season was the American Midwest premiere of the Polish opera *King Roger* by Karol Szymanowski. The Polish community responded with an international outpouring of support.

David Osborne came to MOT in February 1993 as director of production. He instantly became a major and integral force with the company and has produced every single opera since he arrived. This includes every opera presented on the Detroit Opera House stage since its opening in 1996. To date, it adds up to an incredible 108 operas in a row. There have also been several major concerts, as well as his being involved in sixty-two dance presentations. It has been a remarkable run in a critical department, with Mr. Osborne being responsible for everything that the audience sees and hears on the stage, at every performance.

When Mr. Osborne joined MOT in 1993, the opera house was still very much on the drawing board, and he played a key role in determining specifications for

The History of Michigan Opera Theatre   31

Suzanne Mallare Acton and David Osborne at the 2013 Opera Ball

Leona Mitchell as Aida from *Aida* in 1993

the stage house and stage as well as technical needs and operating procedures. He also coordinated key capital improvement projects on the opera house, including completing the decorative painting, restorations of the building facades, and the construction of the Ford Center for Arts and Learning.

The wrecking ball came down on the Roberts Fur Building on the Grand Circus Theatre block in spring 1993, making way for the enormous task of building a new seventy-five-thousand-square-foot stage house. Kim Johnson, former executive director of the Music Hall Center for the Performing Arts, was named managing director of the Detroit Opera House and charged with overseeing the restoration and renovation of the building. With a $1.25 million Kresge Challenge grant, the acquisition of the last of the eight parcels in the Grand Circus Theatre block, and the 1994 Opera Ball inside the unrestored auditorium before a crowd of many who had never seen the interior, the project gained incredible momentum. Construction began in earnest on the stage house during the summer. Opera presentations included *La Bohème*, *The Barber of Seville*, *The Merry Widow*, and *Aida* starring Leona Mitchell.

The Masonic Temple / Fisher Theatre years came to an end with a powerful 1995 spring season that included Mozart's *Don Giovanni* featuring Metropolitan Opera stars Jeffrey Wells and Martile Rowland in an opulent production by the English theatre artist John Pasco. *Swan Lake*, arguably the most popular ballet of all time, was also on the bill, choreographed by Detroit's own Jacob Lascu. The era came to a close with Puccini's beloved *Tosca* starring the famed Russian soprano

Maria Gulegina in the title role. Tremendous enthusiasm was building for the opening of the Detroit Opera House, slated for the spring of 1996. It would be the fulfillment of this company's long-term goal to control its own performance facility, one that would be comparable in function, size, acoustics, and aesthetics with the finest opera houses around the world.

David DiChiera with Mayor Dennis and First Lady Judy Archer at the 1994 Opera Ball

1994 Opera Ball set in the pre-renovation auditorium

The History of Michigan Opera Theatre 33

The Detroit Opera House

The Inaugural Gala at the Detroit Opera House, on April 21, 1996, featuring Luciano Pavarotti making good on his celebrated promise to perform in person, is the single most significant event in the entire history of Michigan Opera Theatre. The dream became a reality as Dame Joan Sutherland declared the Detroit Opera House "open and ready for music." This magnificent theatre was not just a world-class home for the opera company; it also instantly became a cornerstone in the cultural life of the city of Detroit. The mayor, the governor, and the president of the United States all joined the tremendous international outpouring of support for this monumental achievement. Celebrating the company's silver anniversary while opening the beautiful new opera house was both a stunning artistic achievement and a civic contribution of the highest order. DiChiera's dear friend and colleague Lotfi Mansouri, then general director of the San Francisco Opera, wrote to him saying, "You have been a fantastic champion for opera in North America, David, with the commitment, dedication and talent to make the difference. Generations of opera audiences will reap the rewards of your hard work, and that is something to cherish."

The 1996 Spring Season

The spring season included, as the first opera on the opera house stage, *La Bohème* starring Marcello Giordani, followed by Prokofiev's ballet *Romeo and Juliet*,

David DiChiera and Luciano Pavarotti at a press conference before the opening of the Detroit Opera House in 1996

David DiChiera with Chairman Robert Dewar and Dame Joan Sutherland at the Gala Opening of the Detroit Opera House in 1996

La Traviata, and *Salome* featuring Maria Ewing in the title role. The 1996 fall season, aptly named "Building on a Dream," included *Carmen* featuring MOT favorite Irina Mishura, a touring production of *West Side Story*, and a new program, launched by Karen DiChiera, called "Learning at the Opera House," which immediately began winning national awards for its scope and content.

MOT inaugurated its first season of dance at the Detroit Opera House in 1997 with two special presentations by the prestigious American Ballet Theatre. Also on tap were a visit from the Cleveland San Jose Ballet and a third, special program titled "An Extraordinary Evening of Dance." In addition, there were Broadway touring productions of *A Chorus Line* and *Damn Yankees* featuring Jerry Lewis. The year 1997 also featured *Aida*; *Rigoletto*; *The Marriage of Figaro*; MOT's first Wagner opera, *The Flying Dutchman*; and *The Magic Flute*, with set and costume design by Maurice Sendak. World-class maestros Steven Mercurio, Klaus Donath, and John Mauceri were featured on the podium leading the way. MOT was firmly ensconced in its new home, and spectacular programming was the order of the day.

The spring season in 1998 opened with MOT's first-ever staging of Massenet's moving and sensual *Manon* featuring Marcello Giordani and Ruth Ann Swenson, followed by Donizetti's *The Elixir of Love* and George Gershwin's *Porgy and Bess* starring Gordon Hawkins and Marquita Lister. MOT was among the very first opera companies to present *Porgy and Bess*.

Throughout its history, MOT has been very proud to be a leader in seeking out and introducing some of the world's great African American operatic talent. Kathleen Battle, Cleo Lane, Leona Mitchell, Wilhelmina Fernandez, Gregg Baker, and Vinson Cole are but a few of the featured artists and are a reflection of MOT's exemplary history of multicultural casting.

Kathleen Battle as Pamina and Ron Raines as Papageno from *The Magic Flute* in 1977

The History of Michigan Opera Theatre

Also on tap this year were productions of *Turandot* starring Richard Margeson and Alessandra Marc and *Lucia di Lammermoor* starring Sumi Jo, Fernando De La Mora, and Evgenji Dmitriev, along with a *Roméo et Juliette* presented by Le Ballet de Monte Carlo, which included an appearance by the president of the company, H.S.H. Princess Caroline of Monaco.

Spectacular programming continued with American Ballet Theatre's third visit to its "Midwest home," featuring a new production of *Don Quixote* and a touring production of Andrew Lloyd Webber's *Sunset Boulevard* starring Petula Clark. The spring dance season included a visit from the Paul Taylor Dance Company, and the spring opera season featured *Madame Butterfly*, MOT's first production of Tchaikovsky's *Eugene Onegin*, and a magnificent *Samson and Delilah* starring Irina Mishura.

MOT presented the Three Tenors in July 1999, at Detroit's historic Tiger Stadium, in the world-renowned trio's only North American appearance that year. The Three Tenors concert launched MOT's New Century Fund and provided the opportunity to raise the first $14 million. Also, the superstar tenor Andrea Bocelli made his North American opera debut at the Detroit Opera House in Massenet's *Werther*, the first American production to be webcast.

MOT started the new century with stunning back-to-back visits from the legendary Stuttgart Ballet, making its Detroit debut, and American Ballet Theatre, returning to its Midwest home with a new production of *Swan Lake*. The exciting spring opera season included the presentation of two operas never seen on MOT's stage, *Der Rosenkavalier* and *Peter Grimes*, as well as a powerful and moving *Tosca* with Lisa Daltrius and Amy Johnson in the title role and MOT favorites Marcello Giordani and Ian DeNolfo alternating in the role of Cavaradossi. Wonderful programming continued, and the fall featured a return visit from Les Ballets de

David DiChiera with Princess Caroline of Monaco at the command performance of Les Ballets de Monte Carlo in 1998 at the Detroit Opera House

David DiChiera with Andrea Bocelli, Mario Corradi, Denyce Graves, and maestro Steven Mercurio

36   The History of Michigan Opera Theatre

Alfreda Burke, Karen Marie Richardson, the conductor Suzanne Mallare Acton, Alvin Waddles on piano, and Roderick Dixon with the Too Hot Orchestra and Chorus from *Too Hot to Handel* in 2015

Monte Carlo, performing Prokofiev's *Cinderella*, as well as an MOT production of Mozart's *Così Fan Tutte*. The fall season concluded with MOT's production of *La Bohème*, followed by a national tour production of *Rent*, giving Detroit audiences a rare opportunity to experience these related works back-to-back.

MOT marked its thirtieth anniversary season in 2001 by maintaining its place in the top ten of American opera companies by virtue of its now $12 million budget. A year-long celebration of Giuseppe Verdi continued with *La Traviata*, one of his most famous operas, followed by *Falstaff*, his final opera. The spring season came to a close with Offenbach's *The Tales of Hoffman*. The fall season included a revival of the Armenian national opera *Anoush*, which received its American premiere on the MOT stage in 1982. The production received a tremendous outpouring of financial support from the Armenians for *Anoush* Committee and the hundreds of Armenians and friends who contributed their time and resources to the success of this production.

Renovation continued at the opera house, and 2002 marked the opening of the Cadillac Café, located at the Madison Street entrance. It is a cozy, pub-like bistro open to all guests before curtain and after the performance. The year came to a close with a visit from the legendary Bolshoi Ballet, performing *Swan Lake*, and Cincinnati Ballet's *The Nutcracker*, now a holiday tradition. The year also saw MOT's first production of *Too Hot to Handel*, the jazz-gospel Messiah, conducted by Suzanne Mallare Acton. It went on to be a favorite annual holiday tradition at the Detroit Opera House.

The Michigan premiere of the new American opera *Dead Man Walking*, by Jake Heggie, was an especially notable production in 2003. London's *Guardian* newspaper reported at the time that this new opera "makes the most concentrated impact of any piece of American music theatre since *West Side Story*." The opera repertory also included *Don Giovanni*, directed and designed by John Pasco and conducted by MOT regular Steven Mercurio, as well as *Die Fledermaus*, directed by longtime company friend Bernard Uzan and conducted by MOT's own Suzanne Mallare Acton. There was also a *Madame Butterfly* as well as MOT's first production of Verdi's *A Masked Ball*, along with performances by the Alvin Ailey American Dance Theater and a rare North American appearance of the Kirov Ballet, presented on the only stage in Michigan large enough to accommodate its grandeur.

Two major developments occurred in 2004: the first was the completion of the Crowning Achievement Campaign, allowing MOT to begin its final construction phase, which included building the six-story parking center and renovating the office tower on the Broadway Street side of the Detroit Opera House. The second major development was the announcement that R. Jamison (Rick) Williams Jr. was elected chairman of Michigan Opera Theatre's Board of Directors. Mr. Williams serves to the present day as the opera company's chairman, succeeding Ruth and Lynn Townsend (1971–1975), Lynn Townsend (1975–1980), and Robert Dewar (1980–2000).

R. Jamison (Rick) Williams

Michigan Opera Theatre's Board of Directors unanimously elected R. Jamison (Rick) Williams as its new chairman on February 17, 2004. A prominent businessman and civic leader, Mr. Williams is a successful attorney who has a long history of support for the arts and a passion for opera and dance. Mr. Williams followed in the footsteps of his parents, Jamison and Betty Williams, who were ardent and devoted supporters of the opera company and of the arts in Detroit for many years. Mr. and Mrs. Williams played a major role in the early growth and success of Michigan Opera Theatre. Mrs. Williams had a passion for opera that came to be shared with her son: "she taught me how important it was and how important it can be."

Mr. Williams, a member of the American Bar Association, State Bar of Michigan, Oakland County Bar Association, and American Judicature Society, is senior partner and cofounder of Williams, Williams, Ruby & Plunkett. An authority on the financial structuring of business enterprises, mergers, acquisitions, and divestitures, Mr. Williams is primary counsel to numerous corporations in diverse industries. He is also principal owner of several companies, as well as serving as a director of several others. "You know, when I took this job, somebody warned me that I should be careful, that this is a big job. And it turned out to be true. It's bigger than I ever thought. But what they didn't understand is that this is a labor of love. This is my responsibility. And I'm determined to make it work." Now, three decades into the opera company's existence, MOT was welcoming the leadership of the perfect man for the job.

Mr. Williams and his wife, Karen, have supported MOT with their leadership, generosity and vision. They have played a central role in guiding the company through significant challenges. Together, they have championed David DiChiera's

Top: John Packard as Joseph de Rocher and Kristine Jepson as Sister Helen Prejean from *Dead Man Walking* in 2003

Bottom: Karen and Rick Williams at the 2014 MOT Opera Ball

38   The History of Michigan Opera Theatre

David DiChiera with longtime board member Betty Brooks, Denyce Graves, and the composer Richard Danielpour at the *Margaret Garner* premiere in 2005

vision to produce works that connect directly and emotionally with diverse audiences, playing a significant role in many of the company's successes including *Cyrano, Frida, The Passenger,* and *The Tender Land.*

After six years of preparation, MOT hosted the world premiere of *Margaret Garner* on May 7, 2005, the first world premiere to be presented on the Detroit Opera House stage. It is a powerful American opera by the composer Richard Danielpour and the Nobel Laureate Toni Morrison. It starred the internationally renowned soprano Denyce Graves in the title role and was the result of DiChiera's desire to present a culturally appropriate opera as the company's first world premiere on the Detroit Opera House stage. *Margaret Garner*, a project spearheaded by DiChiera, fulfilled MOT's mission to connect with new audiences and build bridges into the community it serves. In the summer of 2005, the National Association of Negro Musicians honored DiChiera for his continued support of African American artists.

The opera repertoire also included *Tosca, The Daughter of the Regiment*, Bellini's bel canto masterpiece *Norma*, and a revival of *La Bohème*. Also on tap was a much-anticipated return of the Kirov Ballet, one of only three U.S. performances that season, with a lavish production of *The Sleeping Beauty*. MOT and the City of Detroit were also proud to host OPERA America's Opera Conference 2005: Diverse Voices. MOT continued in its role as a major cultural presence as opera colleagues worldwide were welcomed to the magnificent Detroit Opera House and exposed to the many treasures of the city of Detroit.

One of the true highlights of 2006 was the opening of the Ford Center for Arts and Learning, which made facilities available to expand the Community Programs and Dance Departments. The Ford Center, on the Broadway Street side of the Detroit Opera House, is made up of the Chrysler Theatre, a flexible black-box performance space for intimate presentations; the Margo V. Cohen Center

Leah Partridge as Roxane and Marion Pop as Cyrano from *Cyrano* in 2007

Torrance Blaisdell as Capucin, Jose Luis Sola as Christian, Leah Partridge as Roxane, Gloria Parker as La Duegne, and Marion Pop as Cyrano from *Cyrano* in 2007.

for Dance, which serves as the nerve center for all dance activities; the David and Marion Handleman Media Studio, designed to support the Community Programs Department with greater facilities, interactive classroom programming, and distance learning; the Lee & Floy Barthel Costume Shop; and the Allesee Dance & Opera Resource Library, which also serves as the MOT Archive.

Cyrano

Without doubt, the highlight of 2007 was MOT's third world premiere, David DiChiera's magnum opus, *Cyrano*. It is a grand romantic opera, to a libretto by DiChiera's longtime colleague Bernard Uzan and orchestrations by Mark Flint. After playing in Detroit, *Cyrano* had successful runs in Philadelphia and Miami. All three cities reported tremendous audience enthusiasm for the work, with standing ovations and a long list of positive audience comments from each city. The critical response was almost universally positive, with headlines such as "DiChiera's Cyrano a Winner by More than a Nose"; "Cyrano Makes Stunning Debut in Detroit"; "A Nose for Melody: David DiChiera Gives Birth to Cyrano at MOT"; "DiChiera Delivers a Lush, Spellbinding 'Cyrano'"; "Philadelphia's 'Cyrano': Actually They Do Make 'Em Like That Any More." The commentary repeatedly used such phrases as "ravishing harmonies," "arching ensembles," and "superb orchestration," with references to "intimate scenes of longing, love and heartbreak." It was a tour de force and unleashed a spectacular outpouring of support. It was also a smashing kickoff to the 2007 season.

This seminal year also included productions of *Turandot*, MOT's first production of Mozart's *The Abduction from the Seraglio*, Gounod's *Romeo and Juliet*, and

The Marriage of Figaro, as well as appearances by American Ballet Theatre, Grand Rapids Ballet's production of *Where the Wild Things Are*, Miami City Ballet, and the Ballet Folklórico de Mexico. The year 2008 featured Michigan Opera Theatre's first production of Bellini's *La Sonnambula*, along with Puccini's *La Rondine* and audience favorites *La Traviata* and *Madame Butterfly*, as well as a return engagement of the powerful *Margaret Garner*, which also toured to Chicago's Auditorium Theater. Also notable in 2008 was the arrival of MOT's newly formed Children's Chorus. The chorus, directed by Suzanne Mallare Acton, presented its first full staging of a children's opera, *The Maker of Illusions*, along with performing in concert and serving as the in-house children's chorus for all mainstage production requirements.

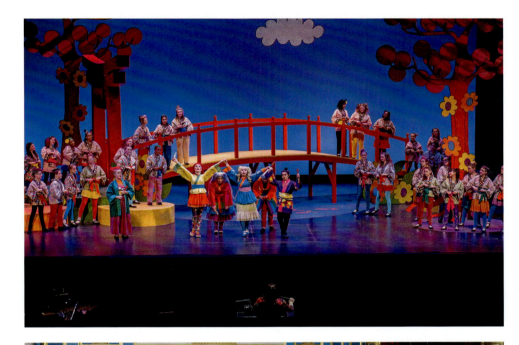

Michigan Opera Theatre's Children's Chorus production of *The Mikado* in 2016

Michigan Opera Theatre's Children's Chorus in 2016

The History of Michigan Opera Theatre 41

With the economy in steep decline in 2007 and 2008, MOT was faced with very serious budgeting issues. In an effort to adjust to the financial realities, the company made a series of dramatic cutbacks. Most notable among the cutbacks was the decision to reduce the opera season by eliminating one opera and going with four operas instead of five. The reduced schedule, along with staffing and other cutbacks, put MOT in a position to move forward and weather the economic downturn.

MOT soldiered on in 2009 with productions of Donizetti's *The Elixir of Love*, the ever-popular *Carmen*, Sondheim's *A Little Night Music*, and a critically acclaimed, spectacular production of Verdi's *Nabucco*, not seen in Detroit since 1961. There were return visits from the American Ballet Theatre, the Grand Rapids Ballet, and the legendary Pilobolus performed on the opera house stage for the first time. *Too Hot to Handel* and *The Nutcracker* were back during the holidays, and the newly formed MOT Children's Chorus undertook children's opera on a larger scale, mounting the Jewish Czech composer Hans Krása's dramatic *Brundibar*.

Continuing MOT's steadfast commitment to quality programming, the 2010 spring opera season featured two treasured opera classics, Mozart's *Don Giovanni* and Puccini's *Tosca*. The spring dance season, featuring two vastly different companies, included a return of the popular Ballet Hispánico and one of Russia's top ballet companies, the Tchaikovsky Ballet, performing *Sleeping Beauty*. In the fall, MOT kicked off its fortieth season of opera with Gilbert and Sullivan's *The Mikado* and the timeless, tragic *La Bohème*. This Puccini favorite featured the MOT debut of the Sardinian tenor Francesco Demuro, alternating with Noah Stewart in the role of Rodolfo, and Kelly Kaduce alternating in the role of Mimi with Grazia Doronzio, who was making her MOT debut following her performance as Liu in *Turandot* at the Met.

Francesca Patane as Abigaille from *Nabucco* in 2009

2011

A more extensive look at 2011 will illuminate the philosophies and practices put in place by Dr. DiChiera long ago and show how they continue to be successful. This somewhat more extensive study will serve as an example of the operating procedures that began forming in the 1970s still holding true in refined form in the twenty-first century and of the way each and every season is carefully calculated and balanced to achieve the most positive effect possible. It is in this way that consistent sustained success, regardless of the financial and economic conditions, has been achieved over the years.

There has been a continuing commitment to scheduling diverse repertoire, including well-known, classic material mixed with more contemporary and American works. Also, using established well-known singers mixed carefully with new faces and including a measure of young, up-and-coming performers in casting has been a DiChiera specialty over the years. As MOT continued its fortieth anniversary season, the company remained committed to the fundamental goals

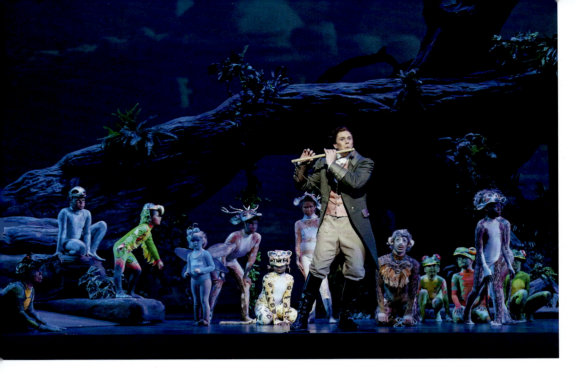

David Miller as Tamino from *The Magic Flute* in 2011

of presenting productions of the highest quality, offering outreach that brings programming to the most diverse audience possible and using the arts to affect the revitalization of the community.

In the spring, there were productions of two audience favorites, *The Magic Flute* and *Rigoletto*. For *The Magic Flute*, the company was excited to bring back the Canadian coloratura soprano Aline Kutan, after her appearance in MOT's 2002 production of *Lakmé*, in which she had garnered praise for her "spectacular ease" and "technical agility." This production also marked the company debut of rising artists, tenors Norman Shankle and David Miller as Tamino and sopranos Katherine Whyte and Ava Pine as Pamina. The season closed with Verdi's *Rigoletto*. The acclaimed American tenor James Valenti returned to MOT to sing the Duke of Mantua, alternating with the Polish tenor Arnold Rutkowski, making his Midwest operatic debut. Returning to the MOT stage, alternating in the title role, were the baritones Todd Thomas and Gaetan Laperriére. The production also featured the company debuts of the sopranos Rachele Gilmore and Sara Joy Miller as Gilda.

In addition, to celebrate MOT's fifteenth season as the home of dance in Detroit, there was a performance by the Alvin Ailey American Dance Theater and the MOT debut of one of the Midwest's premier contemporary dance companies, the Metro Detroit–based Eisenhower Dance Ensemble, in a performance celebrating the iconic Motown sound. Also notable in this spring season was a collaboration with the Rackham Symphony Choir in an evening of Gershwin favorites, featuring the acclaimed Detroit pianist Alvin Waddles, conducted by MOT's Suzanne Acton and featuring the MOT Orchestra.

The 2011 fall season began with a double bill of Menotti's *The Medium* and Orff's *Carmina Burana*, both productions featuring new sets and costumes designed by the Detroit-based, award-winning stage designer Monika Essen. *Carmina Burana* also featured the Eisenhower Dance Ensemble and acrobats from Cirque du Soleil. Returning to the MOT stage for these productions were the

Carmina Burana in 2012

Maggie Allesee receiving the MOT Lifetime Achievement Award from Dr. David DiChiera and Wayne Brown in 2015

up-and-coming young soprano Andriana Chuchman and the dramatic mezzo-soprano Melissa Parks, who appeared together in 2010's *The Mikado*, along with a return by the Romanian baritone Marian Pop, who created the title role in the world premiere of *Cyrano*. In November, there was a return of Mozart's *The Marriage of Figaro*. In this production, MOT welcomed a number of both familiar and new faces, including the company debut of the impressive young conductor Kazem Abdullah. The cast included the baritones Corey McKern and Ian Greenlaw as the philandering Count and the sopranos Rachel Willis-Sorensen and Sian Davies as his wife.

The sixteenth season of dance was made possible by a generous donation by the longtime supporter and company friend Maggie Allesee. Mrs. Allesee was MOT's first $1 million contributor and has been called the most significant advocate for dance in the greater Detroit Metropolitan community. In 2015, Mrs. Allesee was honored with the Michigan Opera Theatre Lifetime Achievement Award in recognition of a lifetime devotion to the arts. Her generosity continues to the present, especially with MOT's dance programming.

The 2011 dance season featured the Detroit premiere of Rasta Thomas's Bad Boys of Dance as well as the return of the annual production of *The Nutcracker*, marking the first performance of the BalletMet Columbus on the opera house stage. The year came to a close with what has become an annual tradition, the audience favorite, jazz-gospel Messiah, *Too Hot to Handel*.

It was truly a year that reflected MOT's philosophies and practices, with a broad array of performances and diverse collection of artists geared to engage the broadest audiences and reach out to the widest possible public. Even in the most difficult economic climate, Dr. DiChiera continued to exercise his unique genius for programming and casting, bringing yet another stellar season to the Detroit Opera House.

With the economy starting to show signs of life, MOT rode out the recession in 2010 and 2011 by hunkering down to meet expense and revenue goals and sticking with a reduced schedule of four instead of five operas for each season. Cost cutting trimmed MOT's budget from $12.5 million to just under $10 million. However, the company was handcuffed by a crushing $18 million bond debt on the opera house and the parking center.

The Legacy Preserved: A Secure Future

Facing the very real probability of bankruptcy, in December 2011, MOT reached agreement with its lenders to cut the long-term debt, provided that MOT pay $11 million by June 30, 2012. Along with the omnipresent Dr. DiChiera, these actions to literally save the company were led by MOT board chairman R. J. "Rick" Williams in what can be described as a monumental effort. It was clearly one of the most critical historical mileposts in the entire history of the company. The Preserve the Legacy Campaign was launched, and MOT raised $7 million. With these funds, the company negotiated a new lease and paid off its former lenders. As a result, MOT became financially sustainable for the foreseeable future. "I cannot overstate the importance of what we've just achieved," DiChiera said at the time. The company had struggled for years with extensive bank debt due to the collapse of the national and local economy. Now with the economic recovery moving forward and the company's restructured debt, DiChiera could look forward to his retirement strategy and laying the groundwork for the next era of his beloved, financially sustainable opera company.

The spring season in 2012 brought a return of Bizet's exotic *The Pearl Fishers*, which featured the wildly colorful designs of the iconic fashion designer Zandra Rhodes as well as the return of the audience favorite Leah Partridge, last seen in the world premiere of *Cyrano*. In May, there was a production of Leoncavallo's

Nmon Ford as Zurga, Leah Partridge as Leila, and Noah Stewart as Nadir from *The Pearl Fishers* in 2012

Chairman Rick Williams

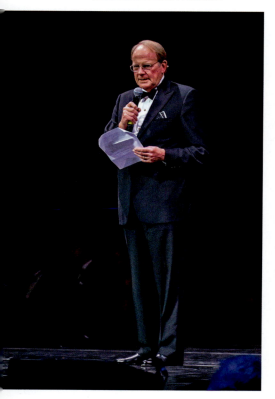

I Pagliacci after a long absence from the MOT stage. The Maggie Allesee Dance Series featured a return of the ever-popular Alvin Ailey American Dance Theater and the North American premiere of Barcelona Ballet's *Swan Lake*. In March was a performance of *Harold and the Purple Crayon* by the contemporary dance company Hubbard Street 2. Also of note, the Michigan Opera Theatre Children's Chorus continued to thrive, with a production of *HMS Pinafore*. MOT is one of the few opera companies in the country to have a permanent ensemble of young people, which is a vital part of the organization's mission to bring cultural enrichment to all the communities they serve. The fall season opened with *The Barber of Seville*, followed by the company's first baroque opera, Handel's *Julius Caesar*. The noted American counter-tenor David Daniels made his company debut in this production. The seventeenth season of "Dance in the D" brought the company debut of New York City Ballet's MOVES as well as a return of BalletMet Columbus's *The Nutcracker*. The year came to a rousing close with the now-traditional performance of *Too Hot to Handel*.

An Opera Hero Plans His Exit

"An Opera Hero Plans His Exit" was the headline in the *Detroit Free Press* on February 3, 2013. The time had come, and after nearly fifty years at the helm, David DiChiera was preparing to retire. MOT announced a national search for a new executive director. DiChiera would move into the position of artistic director, with plans to stay in this capacity until 2017 to aid in the transition to the next era.

46 The History of Michigan Opera Theatre

The tributes poured in, recognizing DiChiera's incomparable achievements. Most notably, DiChiera was recognized by the National Endowment for the Arts at the Kennedy Center as a recipient of its Opera Honors. It is our nation's most prestigious opera award. The general feeling was summarized by Marc Scorca, president of OPERA America: "There is only one David DiChiera on earth. He is the most winning and visionary person I know."

On February 4, 2013, MOT announced its search for a new executive director. There would be an evolution in leadership, in which Dr. DiChiera would transition to the position of full-time artistic director. DiChiera reported that he was thrilled at this stage of his career to be able to step away from the administrative and financial headaches that would fall to the new executive director. "I'm giving myself a gift for the next several years," he said. "I'm going to give myself the pleasure of just worrying about what goes up on the stage."

Mainstage production in 2013 included the Eisenhower Dance Ensemble, the esteemed Dance Theatre of Harlem, the ever-popular Alvin Ailey American Dance Theater, and the Los Angeles–based contemporary dance troupe Diavolo. The spring opera season saw the company premiere of Beethoven's *Fidelio* and the most grand and dramatic spectacle in all opera, Verdi's *Aida*. The fall opera season included a return of Wagner's ghostly romantic opera *The Flying Dutchman* and one of the most performed operas in the world, *La Traviata*, featuring Nicole Cabell, recent winner of the BBC Cardiff Singer of the World Competition.

Aida in 2013

The Great Transition

"David is our founder and has been the visionary leader for everything that has happened at Michigan Opera Theatre for over forty years," said Rick Williams, MOT chairman. "We have always known the day would come when David would want to scale back his responsibilities and that when it does, we would split David's role into two positions, that of an executive director and an artistic director. It has always been too much for one person, but David's a Superman kind of guy, and he always wanted to do it all." Williams reported that he and the board had initial discussions on the search and that he was in the process of organizing a search committee. "David is a beloved figure in our community, and we don't take the job of replacing him—or even half of him—lightly. This has been in our thinking for quite a while," Williams said, "but we didn't want to do anything until we had our financial house in order. We were able to accomplish that with our successful debt restructuring this summer."

The search committee was made up of MOT board members Betty Brooks, Dodie David, Ethan Davidson, Sandy Duncan, David DiChiera, Herman Frankel, Barbara Kratchman, and Al Lucarelli. In light of DiChiera's decision to stay on as artistic director, the committee was able to focus on a nationwide search for a leader with significant background in the art forms of opera, music, and dance, one whose primary attributes were based on demonstrated, successful experience in executive and administrative function in arts organizations. The new leader also had to be committed to building on the historical connection between MOT and the City of Detroit.

In November, MOT named the native Detroiter Wayne S. Brown as its new president and CEO. The news broke on December 6 in the *Detroit Free Press*, where Brown explained that the lure of working with a visionary leader like DiChiera and returning home to Detroit were the deciding factors. The news, of course, was all over the media, and Brown was quoted in a report from the online theater website Encore Michigan saying, "Coming home to Michigan to be part of the city's transformation and to work side-by-side with a legend like David DiChiera is a huge honor for me. It's an opportunity of a lifetime, and I look forward to building on the enormous strides David, the board and the staff have made in making MOT one of the premier opera companies in the United States. I can't wait to get started."

Wayne S. Brown

After graduating from MacKenzie High School in Detroit, Wayne Brown attended the University of Michigan, where he received his bachelor of music degree with a major in voice and a minor in business. He met his wife, Brenda Kee, at the University of Michigan, where she went on to earn her doctor of musical arts degree in piano. After graduating from U of M, Brown went to work for the Detroit

Chairman Rick Williams with new president and CEO Wayne Brown and Dr. David DiChiera

Symphony Orchestra, where among other responsibilities he helped establish the Classical Roots Concerts, which would champion African American composers and bring a general awareness to ethnic diversity in the classical music community. Then it was on to leadership positions with symphony orchestras in Massachusetts and Kentucky, followed by a position in Atlanta as music producer of the Cultural Olympiad for the Olympic Games. From there, beginning in 1997, Brown served as director of music and opera for the National Endowment for the Arts in Washington, D.C. Among his responsibilities was managing the NEA Opera Honors and the NEA Jazz Masters. In addition, Brown was a founding member of the Magic in Music Advisory Board for the John S. and James L. Knight Foundation, has served on advisory boards for the Mellon and Ford Foundations, is a former vice chairman of the American Symphony Orchestra League, and previously served as a member of the American Arts Alliance Board.

In response to Brown's appointment at MOT, Marc Scorca, president of Opera America, said, "The appointment of Wayne Brown as President and CEO of Michigan Opera Theatre is tremendously exciting. Wayne will arrive at the company with an established national reputation, an incomparable knowledge of artistic trends and best management practices, and an unparalleled level of goodwill among his opera colleagues. He has a long-standing commitment to Detroit and its cultural community and will build on the strong foundation laid by David DiChiera." The Great Transition had begun, and MOT was looking forward to a bright sustainable future.

Newly appointed president and CEO Wayne Brown hit the ground running in the spring of 2014, not only planning to preserve the forty-three-year legacy of MOT but also intending to "sustain the vitality and strengthen the future of

President and CEO Wayne Brown at the 2016 MOT Opera Ball

Beverly O'Regan Thiele as Beatrice, Kim Josephson as Eddie, Kiri Deonarine as Catherine, and Eric Margiore as Rodolfo from *A View from the Bridge* in 2014

opera and dance in Southeastern Michigan and beyond." He further stated, "Our shared goal is to continue to make the Detroit Opera House, one of the city's cultural landmarks, a singular destination for artists and inter-generational audiences alike through our organization's goal: defining and creating a sustainable path for exceptional artistic presentations and compelling community and educational programs."

The spring season continued to reflect the programming philosophy that Dr. DiChiera has adhered to for years—presenting a balance of well-known favorites along with works that are new to the MOT audience. The spring dance season brought familiar troupes, the Dance Theatre of Harlem and the Joffrey Ballet, along with the American debut of the celebrated Ballet du Grand Théâtre de Genève in a thrilling program of avant-garde works. The spring opera season included the audience favorite *Turandot* and, in an especially notable development, the Michigan premiere of *A View from the Bridge* by William Bolcom, one of today's most celebrated opera composers and emeritus professor of composition at the University of Michigan. The opera is based on the play by the great American playwright Arthur Miller, who shares a connection to U of M. It was the first installment of a new DiChiera initiative called "Opera of Our Time," a plan to introduce more modern and contemporary operas to the MOT repertory.

A Triumphant Return to a Five-Opera Season

An MOT press release on March 12, 2014, announced the details of the upcoming season and a "triumphant return to a five opera season." After six years of seasons with a reduced schedule of only four operas, due to the extremely difficult economic climate, MOT was able to begin the rebuilding process in earnest. All things considered, it was a triumph, and it was due to the company having achieved financial sustainability by restructuring its debt, a clearly improving economy, and increasing individual, corporate, and foundation support. A bright, sustainable future was at hand, and MOT was moving forward with confidence.

The fall 2014 opera season planned by Dr. DiChiera began with the company premiere of Richard Strauss's horror-filled, signature opera, *Electra*. The internationally acclaimed, Grammy Award–winning soprano Christine Goerke was engaged to sing the title role in all of the performances. The opening night performance began at five p.m. and was immediately followed by MOT's fall gala, the Opera Ball, which was the signature event of a weekend full of activities that reflected the growing support, the enthusiasm, the fund-raising, and the dedicated outreach that were all part of a vigorous effort to grow the company's status and stature in the community. Also included in the opera season were productions of the audience favorite *Madame Butterfly*, Lehar's *The Merry Widow* featuring the world-renowned soprano Deborah Voigt in the title role, and to close the season in May, Gounod's *Faust*.

Christine Goerke as Elektra from 2015 *Elektra*

Frida

In a season full of highlights, the most notable historical development came in March 2015 with MOT's production of Robert Xavier Rodriguez's *Frida*, a contemporary opera that paints a musical portrait of the life of the Mexican artist Frida Kahlo. It was the Midwest premiere of this opera. This was a landmark coproduction with the Macomb Center for the Performing Arts. It was performed at the Macomb Center, as well as at two other partner venues, the Berman Center for the Performing Arts and the Detroit Institute of Arts Detroit Film Theatre. DTE Energy Foundation was the title sponsor of the production, and this support enabled MOT's first mainstage opera production outside the Detroit Opera House, bringing world-class opera experiences of this kind directly to audiences in Macomb and Oakland Counties for the first time. This coproduction marked the beginning of an annual collaboration between MOT and the Macomb Center, and there was an all-out effort by MOT regarding audience building and engagement. A month-long series of special events leading up to the highly anticipated premiere at the Macomb Center featured special presentations at the recently formed opera clubs in Sherwood Forest / Palmer Woods, Macomb County, Rosedale Park, Birmingham/Bloomfield, Grosse Pointe, and Indian Village. Other special events included a Gala Red Carpet Opening event, Complimentary

Ricardo Herrera as Diego Rivera and Catalina Cuervo as Frida from *Frida* in 2015

Preview events, matinee performances, and student/senior-citizen dress rehearsals. All this activity was taking place to be timed perfectly with the documentary *Rivera in America*, televised on WTVS, Channel 56, Detroit Public Television, and the *Diego Rivera and Frida Kahlo in Detroit* exhibition, which was being held at the Detroit Institute of Arts.

Frida was the initial offering in MOT's new initiative of bringing operas into the surrounding communities, to people who may not otherwise have been able to experience this powerful, dramatic art form. It was an intense effort that also included events copresented by three other partner venues, the University of Michigan Museum of Art in Ann Arbor, the Mexicantown Mercado Food Resource and Engagement Center in southwest Detroit, and the Whiting Auditorium in Flint. MOT's president and CEO Wayne Brown declared, "Community engagement is a principal theme for Michigan Opera Theatre. Throughout the opera, *Frida*, these new partnerships reflect a new era for artistic collaboration in Southeastern Michigan." There was an outpouring of support from the Latino community, with *Frida* honorary chairman Juan Manuel Solana Morales, consul of Mexico to Detroit, leading the way and an impressive Friends of Frida committee of supporters from the community. And as is turned out, the production was a critical success, with uniformly positive reviews and headlines such as "Michigan Opera Theatre Brings a Triumphant 'Frida' to the Community," "MOT's Frida Emotional and Dynamic," "Fiery 'Frida' Offers Intensity and Immediacy," and "An Opera to See, and Hear." To top it all off, Detroit City Council member Raquel Castañeda-López invited Wayne Brown and Dr. DiChiera to a City

Council meeting to accept a testimonial resolution honoring MOT's new initiative of bringing opera into communities through *Frida* and all the related events. All of this reflected MOT's enthusiastic, forward-thinking dedication to audience engagement and community outreach. It was a critically important new effort, based on a tremendous legacy of excellence, to build the brand and to further entrench the opera company into the heart and soul of its expanding community. These were truly strategies on which MOT could build a future.

Building on the Legacy

The production of *Frida* points out several of MOT's strengths, practices, and philosophies that have stood the test of time and continue to be effective. The entire effort toward community engagement, while updated for the present, is very similar to the practices that the DiChieras and their staff employed in the 1960s and 1970s to build the company in the first place. From the very beginning, during the Overture to Opera years, a primary goal was always to establish broad grass-roots, community-based support. The Opera in Residence program in the 1970s was just one example of a fundamental effort to expose people from all walks of life and from all around the state to the world of opera. During the company's formative years, MOT became a model of audience-building technique, and now, with the production of *Frida*, the company was relying on these fundamentals, in refined, updated form, to build relationships with an ever-expanding constituency. In addition, *Frida* was the second installment in DiChiera's Opera of Our Time initiative, which was based on the practice of bringing new, relevant works to his audience in a calculated mix with the standard repertoire. This production also highlights yet another DiChiera specialty, which is bringing works related to specific ethnic communities within the MOT audience. He has garnered national recognition for championing opera of the Polish, the Armenian, the African American, and now the Latino community. Once again, DiChiera had brought an opera that reflected and paid homage to the rich ethnic diversity that makes up the MOT community. MOT president and CEO Brown, quoted in the *Frida* program, summarized: "From the earliest days of MOT, this Detroit-based cultural entity, under its founder Dr. David DiChiera, has been committed to inclusion and diversity on stage and in all aspects of the organization's operation."

2015-2016

MOT continued to move forward on virtually every front during the 2015–2016 season, its twentieth season in the Detroit Opera House. In September 2015, MOT launched the first season of its new resident artist program, called the Michigan Opera Theatre Studio. The internationally renowned tenor Richard Leech was appointed director of the new program and would oversee all its activities as well as all of the Community Program initiatives. Six studio artists would engage in

ten months of advanced training and performance opportunities, including mainstage and community productions. With the hiring of Mr. Leech as the new director of the resident artists program, five talented singers, a coach/accompanist, and a new manager of educational and community programs, MOT clearly demonstrated its commitment to the programs that are central to the core of its mission.

The mainstage 2015–2016 season featured two beloved classics, *La Bohème* and the *Magic Flute*, and the company premiere of Verdi's *Macbeth*. Also on the mainstage, as the third installment in the Opera of Our Time series, MOT presented Mieczyslaw Weinberg's rarely performed and recently discovered opera *The Passenger*, which tells the haunting story of the Holocaust on an enormous, multi-leveled set. With sixty-two community partners, panels, and fully twenty-five community events such as "Art after Auschwitz: An Intercultural Panel and Performance," MOT was engaging the greater community, sparking dialogue about war and human rights. Through *The Passenger*, MOT demonstrated the power of art to heal, to bring disparate forces together and represent history in ways that resonate with contemporary issues. Indicative of the overwhelming positive critical response was the review from the *Detroit Free Press*, in which Mark Stryker

reported, "Combined with the stark and chilling beauty of Weinberg's music, a brilliantly conceived production with a two-tiered set—the barracks of the camp shown below and the comfort of the ship depicted above—and a seamless staging based on director David Pounteny's original 2010 production from Bregenz in Austria, the impact of 'The Passenger' is devastating. In 20 years of opera-going in Detroit, I can't remember a more powerful night in the theater."

Following the example of *Frida*, in the spring, Aaron Copland's rarely produced twentieth-century opera *The Tender Land* returned to the Macomb Center and toured the region, including an appearance at Heinz C. Prechter Educational and Performing Arts Center in Taylor, Michigan. *The Tender Land* was a perfect vehicle to feature MOT's new resident artists and was conducted (as was *Frida*) by MOT's Suzanne Mallare Acton. In addition, in March 2016, MOT in collaboration with University Musical Society of Ann Arbor brought American Ballet Theatre's *The Sleeping Beauty* to the Detroit Opera House, featuring the ballet superstar Misty Copeland in a principal role. Overwhelming demand allowed MOT to add a performance and catapulted ticket sales. The production was 85 percent toward its ticket-sale goal five months prior to opening night.

In the midst of all the activity, MOT made the stunning announcement that it had achieved a balanced budget, as well as a surplus, for fiscal year 2015. "The state of our company is sound," said MOT chairman Rick Williams. "Ten years ago, we wondered if the compromised local economy and the massive amount of debt we had would cause the curtain to fall, . . . but after a decade of hard work and transition, I am proud to say that the future is bright." The company cited fiscal prudence, expanded outreach, and new corporate and community partnerships for the positive results. News of the company's fiscal health came at the conclusion of Wayne Brown's first full season as president and CEO and of founder Dr. David DiChiera's transition to artistic director. "All things considered, 2014–2015 was a very good season for MOT and a great launch for our ambitious future plans," said Brown. "The City of Detroit is in a good place, and MOT can benefit from the excitement in and about the city. We're a big part of it, and we aren't going to squander this opportunity."

Angela Theis as Laurie and Joseph Michael Brent as Martin from *The Tender Land* in 2016

FACING PAGE:
Top: Richard Leech, director of resident artist programs

Bottom: *The Passenger* in 2015

Stephen Lord

The Great Transition took another major step with an announcement on November 17, 2016, to the MOT staff. The news was made public the following day, and the *Detroit Free Press* headline read, "Famed Conductor to Succeed MOT Artistic Director DiChiera." President and CEO Wayne Brown reported, "I am delighted to share the news that Stephen Lord has been named Principal Conductor of Michigan Opera Theatre effective immediately." Lord has had a long-term association with MOT spanning many years and has led MOT opera productions on multiple occasions. Brown continued, "We are pleased that he has agreed to join MOT in a titled position as the search for a new MOT Artistic Director continues."

The History of Michigan Opera Theatre 55

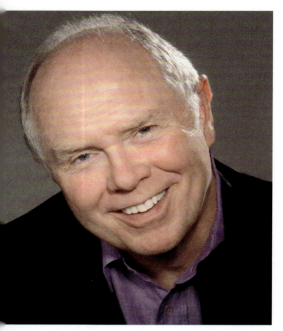

Stephen Lord, MOT principal conductor

Maestro Lord would take a lead role in all artistic matters at MOT, including programming, casting, and auditions, and will work collaboratively with Brown and DiChiera through the end of the 2016–2017 season, when DiChiera assumes the role of artistic director emeritus. "We are delighted that Stephen has agreed to join us and lead us artistically through David DiChiera's transition to an Emeritus position," said Brown.

Stephen Lord has been chosen by *Opera News* as one of the "25 Most Powerful Names in U.S. Opera" (one of four conductors) and is continually praised for conducting both traditional and contemporary operatic works. "Stephen and I have worked together often over the years, and like the rest of the opera world, I have great admiration for the abilities and his creativity. His innate talent and his knowledge and love of opera will be of enormous benefit to MOT," said DiChiera. "I couldn't ask for a better partner to work with during my transition."

The *Detroit Free Press* called Lord "one of the most respected conductors and artistic administrators in American Opera" and pointed out that "Lord's appointment ensures a smooth hand-off as DiChiera departs, while buying MOT more time for its search. It also brings into the fold an artistic leader with the experience, connections and vision to push the company forward, rather than simply tread water for two years."

"I'm thrilled to accept this position with Michigan Opera Theatre," said Lord. "This is a company I've known and respected for a long time, and I have always looked forward to my return visits. Under David and Wayne's leadership, MOT has become one of the premier companies not only in the U.S. but in the world, and I welcome the opportunity to continue and grow the traditions that have been started here." Lord also noted, "David DiChiera is leaving a beautiful legacy, and all of us who love him have to do anything we can to honor his pioneering efforts and to keep it going."

A Bright and Sustainable Future

MOT was building on its solid foundation and moving forward with confidence. It was called The Great Transition by board chairman Rick Williams, and it was fully under way. MOT had achieved sustainability with its renegotiated debt load, and the tremendous legacy put in place over fifty years by the visionary, indefatigable David DiChiera would be preserved. New president and CEO Wayne Brown was firmly ensconced in his leadership role, with the irreplaceable support of company founder DiChiera moving into his role as artistic director emeritus. Now with the naming of Steven Lord as principal conductor, a smooth transition to the new era was assured. There was a triumphant return to a five-opera season with a dedicated eye on outreach, and a new strategic plan to plot the future was in the works. By all indications, MOT was prepared and very much looking forward to a bright and sustainable future.

In the fall of 1971, at the Music Hall, David DiChiera and his young opera company planted the seed that resulted in the rebirth of the theatre and entertainment district in Detroit, a district that at the turn of the twenty-first century was one of the largest in the nation. Beyond the theatre and entertainment district in an even larger context, DiChiera's efforts were an important and significant contribution to the renaissance of the city of Detroit and the cultural life of the greater metropolitan area in general. It was a classic example of citizen initiative working through private enterprise. The Music Hall and the Detroit Opera House stand as monuments to DiChiera's fortitude as an artistic and civic visionary. It is a beautiful legacy. In the first era of the company, the names David DiChiera and Michigan Opera Theatre are completely intertwined, essentially synonymous. He has been the heartbeat for nearly fifty years, and it has indeed been a triumph, of and for regional opera as well as for the renaissance of the city of Detroit.

David DiChiera and Wayne Brown

The History of Michigan Opera Theatre 57

2 The Detroit Opera House

When the Detroit Opera House opened on April 21, 1996, it was called a "Motown Miracle." The impact of MOT's endeavor went far beyond the world of opera; it went to the very foundation of Detroit's renaissance. It was a major economic development for downtown Detroit and put MOT on a par with the Detroit Symphony Orchestra and the Detroit Institute of Arts as a full cultural partner.

It was also called "The House That David Built." As with all things MOT in the first era of this opera company, it was David DiChiera at the center of the action. It was his vision, his persistence, his consummate fund-raising skills, and his ability to build a coalition of support that brought the beautiful facility to reality. "We had no future without a dedicated home for Michigan Opera Theatre. As a tenant, we could not fulfill our destiny of offering world-class opera," DiChiera said at the time.

"The other theatres have served us well, but the MOT Board of Directors has always desired to have our own home," said Robert A. Dewar, board chairman. "The impact is international in scope—singers from the U.S. and from across the world can realize our potential for being a world-class player in the opera scene."

Indeed, MOT's strategic planning had always indicated the need for a house that was devoted to opera. There were two primary issues facing the company. The first was facilities that were simply not big enough to handle all of the requirements of a world-class opera company. The second issue was lack of control of a facilities calendar and having to book dates year to year. In opera, if you want to have an established, international artist, you must be able to make a commitment to that artist sometimes three or four years in advance. So a permanent home with control of the facilities calendar was the goal, and in the late 1980s, the search was on. While exploring Detroit's Theatre District, MOT officials came upon the Grand Circus Theatre. They found it ideal. The Italian Renaissance–style auditorium was modeled after the European opera houses, and DiChiera knew right away that it was right for the company.

In 1989, MOT secured the first parcel on the Grand Circus Theatre block, and in 1990, it was able to purchase the remaining property on the block. MOT bought the theatre with the adjoining office towers, the Roberts Fur building, the International Art building, plus three parking lots. In 1992, Kimberly Johnson was named managing director of the opera house project, and in 1993, the project began in earnest with a ground-breaking that set the renovation into motion.

The building was constructed in 1922 by the legendary theatre architect C. Howard Crane and opened as the Capital Theater. It was Detroit's first movie palace.

Grand Circus Theatre balcony seats after water damage

View of the Grand Circus Theatre's main floor seats out from the stage, before the Detroit Opera House in 1988.

In 1929, the building became the Paramount Theater, and in 1934, the name was changed to the Broadway Capital Theatre. In 1960, the building became the Grand Circus Theater, and in 1985, the facility was closed. It had fallen into complete disrepair, and among many problems and issues, the roof was leaking so badly that it caused tremendous damage to virtually the entire building.

"When I first walked in here six years ago, I felt in awe peering through the rubble and destruction," DiChiera explained, "and I just imagined what the place would look like if it had been maintained. If the owner had cared enough to fix the roof, we would not be re-creating the plaster molds. And if we built a new facility, I doubt you'd be able to match the grandeur and beauty of the main lobby or procure items like back-lit stained glass and chandeliers."

The theatre is crafted in the opera-house style, so it has the best features of the old-world European opera houses. And it would be married with the most efficient and technically advanced production capabilities with a brand-new stage house. It was a unique renovation, combining restoration with new construction. This is a theatre that allows opera to be seen and heard as it was meant to be. Architect C. Howard Crane took care of the acoustics when designing the building for unamplified sound. The acoustical properties of the auditorium are truly splendid and very difficult to duplicate.

60   The Detroit Opera House

Tour of old the Grand Circus Theatre in June 1993

Water damage in the old Grand Circus Theatre lobby in 1995

The Detroit Opera House 61

Right, top: Interior view of Broadway Theatre lobby entrance during renovation

Right, bottom: David DiChiera inspecting theatre renovation in 1994

Below: David DiChiera at the top of grand staircase during renovation in 1994

It was a $28 million renovation and construction project. MOT actually got quite a deal. If it had re-created the opera house from scratch, it was estimated that it would have easily cost $90 to $100 million. Everyone could see the importance of restoring this theatre instead of building new.

Two of the buildings were demolished to make way for the new stage house, lobby, and glass elevator tower. The remaining structure was renovated into dressing rooms, patron services areas, and administrative offices. The renovation included cleaning three, two-thousand-piece crystal chandeliers from the former Czechoslovakia. Other interior features include a grand staircase, Tiffany-style stained-glass panels, frescoes, brass features, marble ornamentation, and marble drinking fountains.

62   The Detroit Opera House

Left: Restoration construction of the theatre, view from the upper balcony in 1995

Below, left: Robert Dewar, David DiChiera, and Kim Johnson in the balcony during theatre renovation in 1996

Below, right: David and Karen DiChiera interviewed in front of the Furs by Robert building before demolition for the stage and receiving addition

Addition of stage and receiving bay to the Detroit Opera House in 1995

The DOH auditorium was returned as closely as possible to its 1922 splendor thanks to blueprints and drawings from the C. Howard Crane architectural records. (Crane also designed the Fox Theatre and Orchestra Hall.) Also instrumental was black-and-white insurance photography taken by the Manning Brothers experts.

While under construction, the site was a blend of old and new technologies. Traditional craftspeople such as masons, carpenters, plasterers, and modelers were everywhere. Also, in order to plaster and paint the ceiling of the theatre, a unique scaffolding was set up that was wired with the same high-tension cable used on U.S. Navy aircraft carriers to snag incoming F-14 fighters.

The Detroit Opera House is a state-of-the-art facility comparable to the world's leading venues of lyric theatre presentation. It features a seventy-five-thousand-square-foot stage house with a lobby, elevator tower, and eighteen grand tier boxes, with mezzanine and balcony seating. Also included are two adjoining office towers, which underwent extensive remodeling to serve as patron service areas and offices for MOT staff, as well as spaces for community programs, a dance studio, a black box theatre space, and a resource library.

The DOH is a marvel for opera lovers. The orchestra pit can hold ninety to a hundred musicians, enough to put on any opera including those by Wagner and Strauss, undoable at any other Detroit venues. Its intimate seating, 2,880 seats in a shallow horseshoe, includes balcony seats that hang just fifty feet from the stage. C. Howard Crane was known for his cantilevered balconies, and the city's first movie palace preceded the talkies and electronic amplification, which gave rise to the excellent acoustics. The stage is seven thousand square feet with a depth of sixty-five feet and an additional forty feet beyond that for storage. The foundation for the stage floor is a fifty-six-foot-wide, post-tensioned monolithic concrete slab and is cantilevered to extend sixteen feet over the orchestra pit. The stage floor is wood, with rubber insulation between it and the concrete slab. The Detroit Opera House became the only venue in this tricounty area that can handle large-scale dance, theatre, and opera works. MOT could now share or trade productions with any of the largest opera-producing venues in the world.

Exterior view of the stage and receiving addition

Interior view from the balcony of the stage and receiving addition

Herman Frankel, board member and parking center champion

In 2005 MOT completed its campus by opening a new parking center just across the street from the opera house. Much of the credit for this goes to longtime supporter and benefactor Herman Frankel. He insisted that the opera house needed a parking center and saw to it, exercising his considerable influence to make it a reality. Mr. Frankel was a major influence in the campaign to restore the opera house and worked closely with Dr. DiChiera on the conception and construction of MOT's permanent home. In the year 2002, thanks to the commitment of Mr. Frankel and with the support of the Board of Directors, MOT completed the purchase of an adjacent garage, and in 2005, the grim old garage was replaced with a striking new parking center.

The opening of the Detroit Opera House was a shining symbol of Detroit's renaissance. The MOT story demonstrates Detroit's can-do spirit. A city landmark was saved and lovingly returned to its 1922 splendor, bringing a sense of vitality and promise to an area with much potential. There was an unmistakable sense of pride that Detroit would finally have a world-class opera house.

TECHNICAL SPECIFICATIONS OF THE DETROIT OPERA HOUSE

Seating capacity = 2,880

Proscenium = 20' high × 53.4' wide

Stage dimensions = 110' wall to wall × 65' deep

Upstage wing space = 53' wide × 38' deep

Rehearsal studio / black box performance space = 66' wide × 54' deep

Dressing room space for 80 performers

Orchestra pit has two elevators and can accommodate up to 100 musicians

Covered, fenced loading dock for two 53' trailers

87 line sets, 1,950 lbs. arbor capacity

Grid to deck = 85'

Stage power

    Three 400 amp company switches

    Four 200 amp company switches

    One 200 amp isolated company switch for sound

    One 200 amp company switch on dock for bus power

480 ETC Sensor dimmers controlled by ETC Ion board

Three Robert Julian 4.5° Aramis followspots

Full house communication and headset system

Williams hearing impaired system

Wardrobe room with two washers and dryers

"Detroit has a bona fide, beautiful opera house."

Luciano Pavarotti, April 21, 1996

View of Detroit Opera House Box Office and Parking Center on Broadway

Aerial night view of opera house parking center from the Detroit Opera House SkyDeck

"A splendid hall!"

New York Times, December 5, 1997

The Detroit Opera House   67

There was, for the first time in a long while, a sense that the city was dynamic and that it was coming back. People realized that the opera house was part of that and that it would help anchor another section of downtown. By adapting and restoring what was at the time a seventy-year-old theatre, MOT continued its role as a major force for the economic revival of the city of Detroit. At the time,

"The beauty of the Detroit Opera House is easily appreciated when standing in the lobby or sitting in the seats watching a performance."

Newsweek, December 18, 1997

Architectural detail of the Detroit Opera House on Broadway

Day view of the Detroit Opera House on Broadway

"Glory, Glory, Glory"

Tony Randall, October 6, 1996

68   The Detroit Opera House

DiChiera was quoted saying, "The important thing is to get people to come down here, into the city. If they do that, the prospects for the house, and for the city, are very good."

As it turned out, the prospects for both the city and the opera house were very good indeed. At this writing, twenty years after the opera house opened, downtown and midtown, with the theatre and entertainment district nestled in between, are all thriving. People are not only coming to visit and go to events, but they are also moving back downtown in significant numbers—so much so that housing has become scarce. The growth and enthusiasm for being in the city is nothing short of amazing, and without question, the opening of the Detroit Opera House in April 1996 was a fundamental catalyst. Both Michigan Opera Theatre and the renaissance of the city of Detroit are the beneficiaries of David DiChiera's vision and persistence. He ignited a spark that evolved into a civic contribution of the highest order, one that will have lasting effects for generations to come.

Top: Interior shot of the grand staircase and main lobby, from upper balcony

Bottom: Balcony view of the auditorium

"This new part of the second-largest working theatre district in the country assures that Detroit will stay in the forefront of urban areas in terms of our cultural offerings."

Mayor Dennis W. Archer,
April 20, 1996

The Detroit Opera House 69

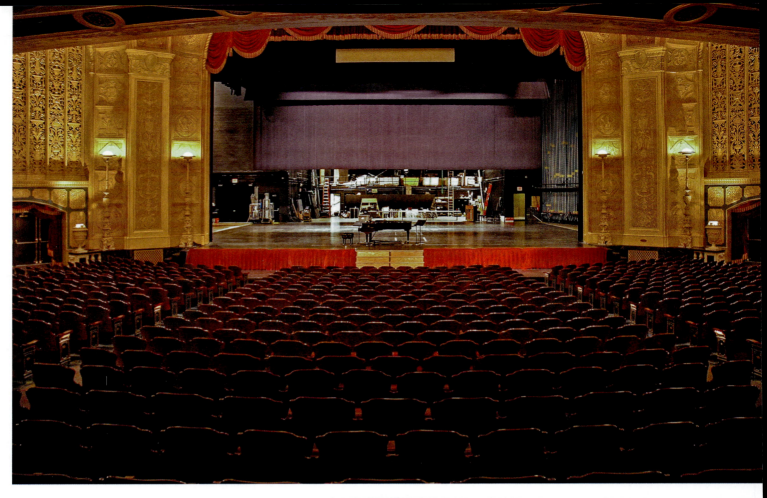

Main floor view of DOH auditorium and stage

The Detroit Opera House

"Both MOT and this wonderful new opera house will prove to be an enduring source of pride for the people of Michigan and for our entire nation."

President Bill Clinton, January 17, 1996

3 The Operas

1970

The Barber of Seville

1971-1972

Joseph and the Amazing Technicolor Dreamcoat
La Rondine
The Perfect Fool

1972-1973

Così Fan Tutte
Tosca
The Telephone and The Medium

1973-1974

Rigoletto
Madame Butterfly
The Merry Widow

1974-1975

La Traviata
Boris Godunov
The Elixir of Love
Die Fledermaus

1975-1976

Porgy and Bess
La Bohème
Lucia di Lammermoor
The Barber of Seville

1976-1977

Washington Square (world premiere)
Madame Butterfly
Naughty Marietta
The Magic Flute

1977-1978

Regina
Carmen
The Student Prince
Faust
Amahl and the Night Visitors

1978-1979

The Pearl Fishers
Show Boat
La Traviata
I Pagliacci and The Emperor Jones
The Tender Land (Midland)
Madame Butterfly (Midland)

1979-1980

The Most Happy Fella
Il Trovatore
La Bohème
Joan of Arc

1980-1981

Die Fledermaus
Of Mice and Men
Don Giovanni
Rigoletto
Fidelio (with Detroit Symphony Orchestra)
The Pearl Fishers (Midland)

1981-1982

Tosca
Carmen
Anoush (American premiere)
The Mikado
Porgy and Bess

1982-1983

The Haunted Castle (American premiere)
Lucia di Lammermoor
Treemonisha
The Marriage of Figaro
The Sound of Music

1983-1984

La Traviata
Faust
A Little Night Music
Anna Bolena

1984-1985

The Merry Widow
The Magic Flute
Sweeney Todd
Aida

1985-1986

Gianni Schicci and I Pagliacci
Martha
West Side Story
Turandot

1986-1987

Orpheus in the Underworld
Madame Butterfly
My Fair Lady
Tosca
The Barber of Seville
Porgy and Bess

1987-1988

Falstaff
Man of La Mancha
Kismet
Il Trovatore
Die Fledermaus
La Bohème
Pavarotti in Concert

1988-1989

The Ballad of Baby Doe
Follies
The Pirates of Penzance
Norma
The Marriage of Figaro
Carmen
Orlando

1989-1990

Les Misérables
Hansel and Gretel
Don Giovanni
La Traviata
Romeo and Juliet

1990-1991

Rigoletto
Show Boat
Ariadne auf Naxos
The Magic Flute
Madame Butterfly

1991-1992

Pavarotti in Concert
Candide
The Mikado
King Roger
Samson and Delilah
Lucia di Lammermoor

1992-1993

Side by Side by Sondheim
The Music Man
La Bohème
Aida

1993-1994

The Barber of Seville
The Merry Widow
Turandot
Faust

1994-1995

Madame Butterfly
The Daughter of the Regiment
Don Giovanni
Tosca

1996

Gala concert for the opening of
    the Detroit Opera House
La Bohème
La Traviata
Salome

1996-1997

Carmen
Rigoletto
The Marriage of Figaro
The Flying Dutchman

1997-1998

Aida
The Magic Flute
Manon
The Elixir of Love
Porgy and Bess

1998-1999

Turandot
Lucia di Lammermoor
Madame Butterfly
Eugene Onegin
Samson and Delilah
The Three Tenors Concert
    (Tiger Stadium)

1999-2000

The Barber of Seville
Werther
Der Rosenkavalier
Tosca
Peter Grimes

2000-2001

La Bohème
Così Fan Tutte
La Traviata
Falstaff
Tales of Hoffmann

2001-2002

Carmen
Anoush
Otello
Lakmé
Marriage of Figaro

72   The Operas

2002-2003

Il Trovatore
Don Pasquale
Don Giovanni
Die Fledermaus
Dead Man Walking

2003-2004

A Masked Ball
Madame Butterfly
The Magic Flute
The Pirates of Penzance
The Pearl Fishers

2004-2005

Rigoletto
Faust
Tosca
Margaret Garner
   (world premiere)
The Daughter of the Regiment

2005-2006

Norma
La Bohème
Aida
Cinderella
Salome

2006-2007

Porgy and Bess
The Barber of Seville
Turandot
The Abduction from the Seraglio
Romeo and Juliet

2007-2008

Cyrano (world premiere)
The Marriage of Figaro
La Sonnambula
La Rondine
La Traviata

2008-2009

Margaret Garner
Madame Butterfly
The Elixir of Love
Carmen

2009-2010

Nabucco
A Little Night Music
Don Giovanni
Tosca

2010-2011

The Mikado
La Bohème
The Magic Flute
Rigoletto

2011-2012

The Medium and *Carmina Burana*
The Marriage of Figaro
The Pearl Fishers
I Pagliacci

2012-2013

The Barber of Seville
Julius Caesar
Fidelio
Aida

2013-2014

The Flying Dutchman
La Traviata
A View from the Bridge
Turandot

2014-2015

Elektra
Madame Butterfly
Frida
The Merry Widow
Faust

2015-2016

La Bohème
The Passenger
The Tender Land
Macbeth
The Magic Flute

2016-2017

Carmen
Silent Night
Little Women
The Girl of the Golden West
Cyrano

A Gallery of Selected Images

Above, left: Robert Monroe as Sporting Life and Leona Mitchell as Bess from *Porgy & Bess* in 1975

Above, right: George Massey as Dr. Falke, Imogene Coca as Prince Orlofsky, and Charles Roe as Gabriel von Eisenstein from *Die Fledermaus* in 1980

Right: Glenda Kirkland as Micaela and Barry Busse as Don Jose from *Carmen* in 1981

Gregg Baker as Crown and cast from *Porgy & Bess* in 1982

James Morris as Henry VIII from *Anna Bolena* in 1984

Cleo Laine as Hanna Glawari from *The Merry Widow* in 1984

Donnie Ray Albert as Porgy and Henrietta Davis as Bess from *Porgy & Bess* in 1987

Dame Joan Sutherland as Norma from *Norma* in 1989

Jeffrey Bruce as The Witch from *Hansel and Gretel* in 1989

Alessandra Marc as Ariadne
from *Ariadne auf Naxos* in 1991

Ruth Ann Swenson as Lucia
from *Lucia di Lammermoor*
in 1992

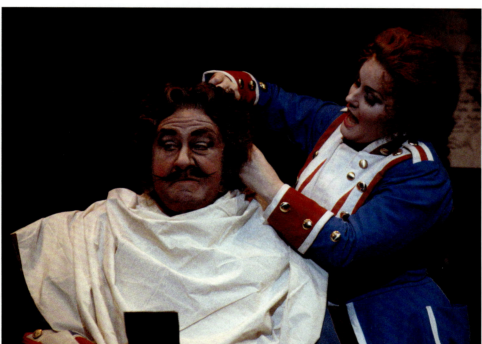

Above, left: Janet Williams as Rosina and Ara Berberian as Don Basilio from *The Barber of Seville* in 1993

Above, right: Pablo Elvira as Figaro from *The Barber of Seville* in 1993

Left: Thomas Hammons as Sulpice and Tracy Dahl as Marie from *The Daughter of the Regiment* in 1994

Above, left: Maria Guleghina as Tosca and Richard di Renzi as Cavaradossi from *Tosca* in 1995

Above, right: Kallen Esperian and Luciano Pavarotti from the 1996 Detroit Opera House Gala Opening

Right: Irina Mishura as Carmen and Richard di Renzi as Don Jose from *Carmen* in 1996

Above, left: Mignon Dunn as Herodias from *Salome* in 1996

Above, right: Irina Mishura as Amneris from *Aida* in 1997

Left: Ruth Ann Swenson as Manon and Marcello Giordani as Chevalier Des Grieux from *Manon* in 1998

The Operas 81

Janet Williams as Adina from *The Elixir of Love* in 1998

Alessandra Marc as Turandot from *Turandot* in 1998

FACING PAGE:
Top, left: Sumi Jo as Lucia from *Lucia di Lammermoor* in 1998

Top, right: Mark Lundburg as Samson from *Samson & Delilah* in 1999

Bottom: Michele Bianchini as Don Basilio, Donato Di Stefano as Don Bartolo, Mary Callaghan Lynch as Berta, Earle Patriarco as Figaro, Bruce Fowler as Count Almaviva and Vivica Genaux as Rosina from *The Barber of Seville* in 1999

82   The Operas

Above, left: Denyce Graves as Charlotte and Andrea Bocelli as Werther from *Werther* in 1999

Above, right: Margaret Lattimore as Octavian and Helen Donath as the Marschallin from *Der Rosenkavalier* in 2000

Right: Marcello Giordani as Caravadossi and Lisa Daltirus as Floria Tosca from *Tosca* in 2000

Mark Baker as Peter Grimes from *Peter Grimes* in 2000

Vinson Cole as Hoffmann from *Tales of Hoffmann* in 2001

The Operas 85

Factory workers and men's chorus from *Carmen* in 2001

Mark Delavan as Iago and Vladimir Galouzine as Otello from *Otello* in 2002

Left: Donato di Stefano as Don Pasquale from *Don Pasquale* in 2002

Below, left: Mary Dunleavy as Donna Anna and Gino Quilico as Don Giovanni from *Don Giovanni* in 2003

Below, right: James Patterson as the Commendatore, Gino Quilico as Don Giovanni, and Kyle Ketelsen as Leporello from *Don Giovanni* in 2003

Above, left: Sarah Coburn as Adele and Robert Orth as Gabriel von Eisenstein from *Die Fledermaus* in 2003

Above, right: Kristine Jepson as Sister Helen Prejean and John Packard as Joseph de Rocher from *Dead Man Walking* in 2003

Right: Ewa Podles as Ulrica from *A Masked Ball* in 2003

Left: Eduardo Villa as King Gustavo and Ewa Podles as Ulrica from *A Masked Ball* in 2003

Below, left: Jeffrey Springer as Pinkerton and Liping Zhang as Cio-Cio-San from *Madame Butterfly* in 2003

Below, right: Liping Zhang as Cio-Cio-San from *Madame Butterfly* in 2003

The Operas 89

Gregory Turay as Tamino and Gloria Parker, Alison Buchanan, and Melissa Parks as the Three Ladies from *The Magic Flute* in 2004

David Gagnon as Frederic, Joyce Campana as Ruth, and cast from *The Pirates of Penzance* in 2004

90   The Operas

Nathan Gunn as Zurga and William Burden as Nadir from *The Pearl Fishers* in 2004

Maureen O'Flynn as Leila, William Burden as Nadir, David Michael as Nourabad, and cast from *The Pearl Fishers* in 2004

The Operas 91

Gordon Hawkins as Rigoletto and Ying Huang as Gilda from *Rigoletto* in 2004

Gordon Hawkins as Rigoletto from *Rigoletto* in 2004

FACING PAGE:
Top: Kyle Ketelsen as Mephistopheles, Pamela Armstrong as Marguerite, and William Burden as Faust from *Faust* in 2004

Bottom: Ines Salazar as Floria Tosca and Yu Qiang Dai as Cavaradossi from *Tosca* in 2005

The Operas 93

Above, left: Gregg Baker as Robert Garner and Denyce Graves as Margaret Garner from *Margaret Garner* 2005

Above, right: Gregg Baker as Robert Garner, Denyce Graves as Margaret Garner, and cast from *Margaret Garner* in 2005

Right: Anita Johnson as Marie and Peter Strummer as Sergeant Sulpice from *The Daughter of the Regiment* in 2005

94   The Operas

Rodrick Dixon as Tonio, Tracy Dahl as Marie, and Peter Strummer as Sergeant Sulpice from *The Daughter of the Regiment* in 2005

Hasmik Papian as Norma, Arutjun Kotchinian as Oroveso, and cast from *Norma* in 2005

The Operas 95

Charles Castronovo as Rodolfo and Liping Zhang as Mimi from *La Bohème* in 2005

Valerian Ruminski as King of Egypt, Salvatore Licitra as Radames, Irina Mishura as Amneris, and Indra Thomas as Aida from *Aida* in 2006

96 The Operas

Above, left: Vivica Genaux as Cinderella and Kenneth Tarver as Don Ramiro from *Cinderella* in 2006

Above, right: Greer Grimsley as Jokanaan and Marquita Lister as Salome from *Salome* in 2006

Left: Gordon Hawkins as Porgy and ensemble from *Porgy and Bess* in 2006

Dalibor Jenis as Figaro and Manuela Custer as Rosina from *The Barber of Seville* in 2006

Turandot in 2007

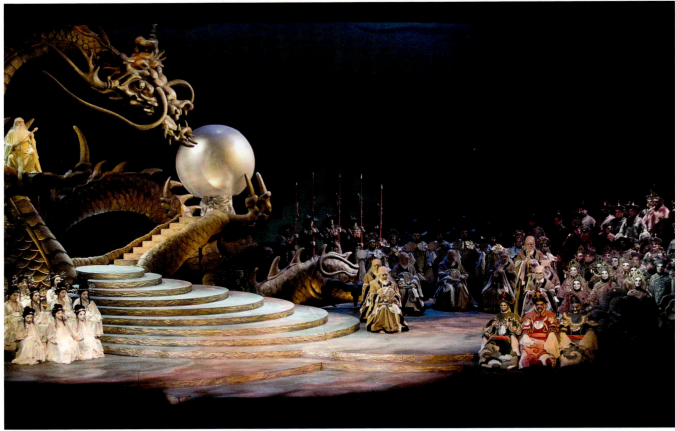

98   The Operas

Elizabeth Futral as Konstanze, Shawn Mathey as Belmonte, and Gregory Frank as Osmin from *The Abduction from the Seraglio* in 2007

Dina Kuznetsova as Juliet and Arturo Chacón-Cruz as Romeo from *Romeo and Juliet* in 2007

Right: Marion Pop as Cyrano and Leah Partridge as Roxane from *Cyrano* in 2007

Below, left: Kathleen Segar as Marcellina, Torrance Blaisdell as Don Basilio, Ying Huang as Susanna, and Robert Gierlach as Figaro from *The Marriage of Figaro* in 2007

Below, right: Ekaterina Siurina as Amina from *La Sonnambula* in 2008

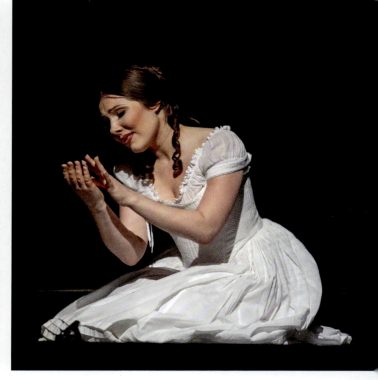

100   The Operas

Victor Ryan Robertson as Prunier, Amanda Squitieri as Lisette, Pamela Armstrong as Magda, and David Pomeroy as Ruggiero from *La Rondine* in 2008

Dina Kuznetsova as Violetta from *La Traviata* in 2008

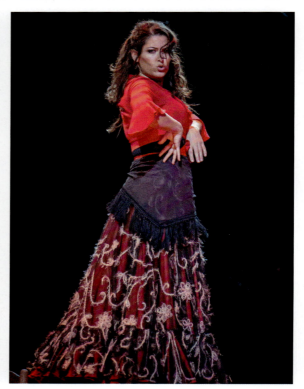

102   The Operas

Top: Alexa Lokensgard as Anna, Burak Bilgili as Zaccaria, Carla Dirlikov as Fenena, and Marco di Felice as Nabucco from *Nabucco* in 2009

Bottom: Alexa Lokensgard as Anna, Burak Bilgili as Zaccaria, and Carla Dirlikov as Fenena from *Nabucco* in 2009

FACING PAGE:
Top, left: Gregg Baker as Robert Garner and Denyce Graves as Margaret Garner from *Margaret Garner* in 2008

Top, right: James Westman as Edward Gaines and Denyce Graves as Margaret Garner from *Margaret Garner* in 2008

Bottom, left: Stephen Costello as Nemorino and Burak Bilgili as Doctor Dulcamara from *The Elixir of Love* in 2009

Bottom, right: Kate Aldrich as Carmen from *Carmen* in 2009

Above, left: Edward Watts as Carl-Magnus, Lisa Vroman as Charlotte, Leslie Uggams as Desiree, and Ron Raines as Fredrik from *A Little Night Music* in 2009

Above, right: Kelly Kaduce as Donna Elvira, Robert Gierlach as Don Giovanni, and Burak Bilgili as Leporello from *Don Giovanni* in 2010

Right: Antonello Palombi as Cavaradossi, Mary Elizabeth Williams as Floria Tosca, Edward Hanlon as Sciarrone, and Todd Thomas as Scarpia from *Tosca* in 2010

Andriana Churchman as Yum-Yum, Michael Wanko as Ko-Ko, and David Curry as Nanki-Poo from *The Mikado* in 2010

Andrew Gray as Colline, Lee Gregory as Schaunard, Kelly Kaduce as Mimi, Kimwana Donor as Musetta, Francesco Demuro as Rodolfo, and Marion Pop as Marcello from *La Bohème* in 2010

Rachele Gilmore as Gilda and Todd Thomas as Rigoletto from *Rigoletto* in 2011

Carmina Burana in 2011

106   The Operas

Rachel Willis-Sorensen as Countess Almaviva, Lauren McNeese as Cherubino, and Grazia Doronzio as Suzanna from *The Marriage of Figaro* in 2011

Jill Gardner as Nedda and Antonello Palombi as Canio from *I Pagliacci* in 2012

René Barbera as Count Almaviva, Elizabeth DeShong as Rosina, and Rodion Pogossov as Figaro from *The Barber of Seville* in 2012

David Daniels as Julius Caesar from *Julius Caesar* in 2012

108   The Operas

Above, left: Angela Theis as Marzellina and Christine Goerke as Leonora from *Fidelio* in 2013

Above, right: Thomas Gazheli as the Dutchman, Burak Bilgili as Daland, and Lori Phillips as Senta from *The Flying Dutchman* in 2013

Left: Nicole Cabell as Violetta and Leonardo Caimi as Alfredo from *La Traviata* in 2013

Kiri Deonarine as Catherine and Kim Josephson as Eddie from *A View from the Bridge* in 2014

Mark Vondrak as Emperor Altoum, Lise Lindstrom as Princess Turandot, and Giancarlo Monsalve as Calaf from *Turandot* in 2014

Christine Goerke as Elektra and Thomas Gazheli as Orest from *Elektra* in 2014

Inna Los as Cio-Cio-San from *Madame Butterfly* in 2014

112 The Operas

Top: Russell Thomas as Faust and Caitlin Lynch as Marguerite from *Faust* in 2015

Bottom: Rodion Pogossov as Marcello, Sean Panikkar as Rodolfo, Marina Costa-Jackson as Musetta, Nicole Cabell as Mimi, Brent Michael Smith as Colline, and Jeff Byrnes as Schaunard from *La Bohème* in 2015

FACING PAGE:
Top, left: Catalina Cuervo as Frida Kahlo from *Frida* in 2015

Top, right: Ricardo Herrera as Diego Rivera and Catalina Cuervo as Frida from *Frida* in 2015

Bottom, left: Deborah Voigt as Hanna Glawari and Roger Honeywell as Count Danilo Danilovitch from *The Merry Widow* in 2015

Bottom, right: Deborah Voigt as Hanna Glawari and ensemble from *The Merry Widow* in 2015

The Operas   113

The ensemble from *The Passenger* in 2015

Adrienn Miksch as Marta, Daveda Karanas as Liese, and Marion Pop as Tadeusz from *The Passenger* in 2015

Joseph Michael Brent as Martin and Angela Theis as Laurie from *The Tender Land* in 2016

Susanna Branchini as Lady Macbeth from *Macbeth* in 2016

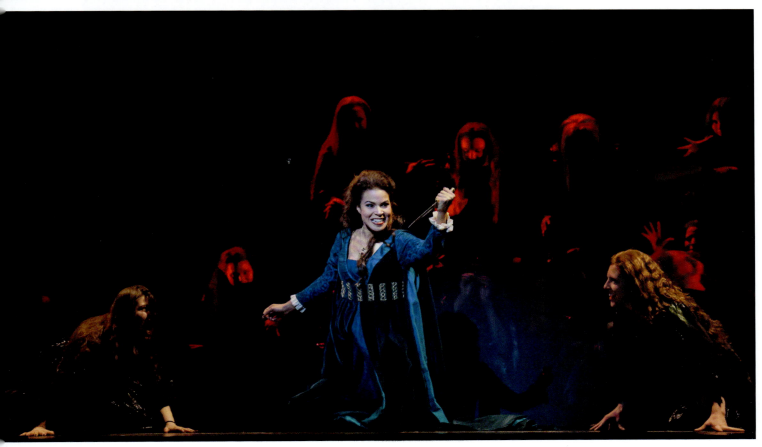

The Operas   115

Gordon Bintner as Papageno, Joshua Dennis as Tamino, the Three Spirits, and the Three Ladies from *The Magic Flute* in 2016

The run of David DiChiera's *Cyrano* was a fitting way to conclude the 2016–2017 season and the end of the era. Marion Pop returned to sing the title role.

116   The Operas

Appendix 1: MOT Donor Honor Roll

Michigan Opera Theatre has gratefully acknowledged the following generous donors for their cumulative lifetime giving. Their support has played a key role in the establishment of Michigan Opera Theatre since its founding in 1971 and in the renovation of the Detroit Opera House. Their leadership has and continues to play an integral part in the company's viability, underwriting quality opera and dance performances, alongside award-winning community and educational programs. Donors such as these are the lifeblood of any arts institution. This listing represents the thousands of donors over the years that have made MOT possible. All donors are listed in every program book, and a complete scanned collection of these program books can be found at MOT's Resource Library website.

$10,000,000 and above

Ford Motor Company

$7,500,000 and above

General Motors Foundation
Michigan Council for Arts and Cultural Affairs

$5,000,000 and above

Fiat Chrysler Automobiles US LLC
The Kresge Foundation

$2,000,000 and above

Mr. and Mrs. Douglas Allison
Mr. and Mrs. Lee Barthel
Community Foundation for Southeast Michigan
William Davidson Foundation
John S. and James L. Knight Foundation
Lear Corporation McGregor Fund
The Skillman Foundation
The State of Michigan

$1,000,000 and above

Mr. and Mrs. Robert A. Allesee
Mr. and Mrs. Eugene Applebaum
AT&T
Bank of America
Mandell & Madeleine Berman Foundation
Mr. and Mrs. John A. Boll, Sr.
DTE Energy Foundation
Margo Cohen Feinberg and Robert Feinberg
Mrs. Barbara Frankel and Mr. Ronald Michalak
Mr. and Mrs. Herman Frankel
Samuel and Jean Frankel
Hudson-Webber Foundation
JPMorgan Chase
Masco Corporation
National Endowment for the Arts
Mr. and Mrs. R. Jamison Williams
Mrs. Sam Williams
Matilda R. Wilson Fund

Appendix 2: MOT Dance Productions

1990

Cleveland San Jose Ballet, *Swan Lake*

1991

Cleveland San Jose Ballet, *Coppélia*

1993

Michigan Opera Theatre, *Sleeping Beauty*

1994

Michigan Opera Theatre, *Cinderella*

1995

Michigan Opera Theatre, *Swan Lake*

1996

Michigan Opera Theatre, *Romeo and Juliet*

1996-1997

American Ballet Theatre, *Swan Lake*
Cleveland San Jose Ballet, *Blue Suede Shoes*

1997-1998

Pittsburgh Ballet Theatre, *Dracula*
American Ballet Theatre, *Giselle*
Alvin Ailey American Dance Theater

1998-1999

Les Ballets de Monte Carlo, *Romeo et Juliette*
American Ballet Theatre, *Don Quixote*
Paul Taylor Dance Company

1999-2000

Ballet Hispánico
Stuttgart Ballet
American Ballet Theatre, *Swan Lake*

2000-2001

Les Ballets de Monte Carlo, *Cinderella*
Alvin Ailey American Dance Theater
American Ballet Theatre, *The Merry Widow*
Les Ballets Trockadero de Monte Carlo
Joffrey Ballet

2001-2002

Tango Pasión
Ballet Internationale, *The Nutcracker*
Dance Theatre of Harlem
Joffrey Ballet
American Ballet Theatre, *Le Corsaire*

2002-2003

Georgian State Ballet
Bolshoi Ballet
Cincinnati Ballet, *The Nutcracker*
Alvin Ailey American Dance Theater
Joffrey Ballet

2003-2004

Kirov Ballet, *La Bayadère*
Cincinnati Ballet, *The Nutcracker*
Dance Theatre of Harlem
Les Ballets Africains
North Carolina Dance Theatre, *Streetcar Named Desire*

2004-2005

National Ballet of Canada, *The Four Seasons, Firebird*
Joffrey Ballet, *The Nutcracker*
A Celebration of Contemporary African-American Dance
Dayton Contemporary Dance Company
Philadanco
Alonzo Kings LINES Ballet
Les Ballets de Monte Carlo, *Cinderella*

2005-2006
Kirov Ballet, *The Sleeping Beauty*
Savion Glover, *Classical Savion*
Joffrey Ballet, *The Nutcracker*
Les Grands Ballets Canadiens de Montréal
Alvin Ailey American Dance Theater

2006-2007
The Royal Winnipeg Ballet, *Dracula*
Joffrey Ballet, *Swan Lake*
Grand Rapids Ballet, *Where the Wild Things Are*

2007-2008
Ballet Folklórico de Mexico
Miami City Ballet, *Agon, Raymonda Variations*
Alvin Ailey American Dance Theater
Joffrey Ballet, *Giselle*
Grand Rapids Ballet, *Peter Pan*

2008-2009
Hubbard Street Dance, *Chicago*
Joffrey Ballet, *The Nutcracker*
Alvin Ailey American Dance Theater
Grand Rapids Ballet, *Aladdin*
American Ballet Theatre, *Romeo and Juliet*

2009-2010
Pilobolus
The Cincinnati Ballet, *The Nutcracker*
Ballet Hispánico
Tchaikovsky Ballet, *Sleeping Beauty*

2010-2011
Grand Rapids Ballet, *The Nutcracker*
Joffrey Ballet
Alvin Ailey American Dance Theater
Eisenhower Dance Ensemble, *Motown in Motion*

2011-2012
Bad Boys of Dance
BalletMet Columbus, *The Nutcracker*
Alvin Ailey American Dance Theater
Corella Ballet, *Swan Lake*

2012-2013
NYC Ballet Moves
BalletMet Columbus, *The Nutcracker*
Eisenhower Dance Ensemble, *Red, Hot & Blue*
Dance Theatre of Harlem
Alvin Ailey American Dance Theater

2013-2014
Diavolo
BalletMet Columbus, *The Nutcracker*
Dance Theatre of Harlem
Joffrey Ballet
Ballet du Grand Théâtre de Genève

2014-2015
Houston Ballet, *Giselle*
BalletMet Columbus, *The Nutcracker*
Alvin Ailey American Dance Theater

2015-2016
BalletMet Columbus, *The Nutcracker*
Eisenhower Dance Ensemble
Dance Theatre of Harlem
American Ballet Theatre, *Sleeping Beauty*

2016-2017
Mark Morris Dance Group
BalletMet Columbus, *The Nutcracker*
Batsheva Dance Company
Eisenhower Dance with State Street Ballet
Royal Winnipeg Ballet, *The Cinderella Story*
Alvin Ailey American Dance Theater

Appendix 3: MOT Premieres

1967

The Portuguese Inn by
 Luigi Cherubini
Libretto by Giulio Confalonieri
English text by John Gutman
Michigan premiere

1969

Der Jasager by Kurt Weill
Libretto by Bertolt Brecht
Midwest premiere

1971

Help, Help the Globolinks by
 Gian Carlo Menotti
Midwest premiere

*Joseph and the Amazing
 Technicolor Dreamcoat* by
 Andrew Lloyd Weber
Lyrics by Tim Rice
Michigan premiere

La Rondine (The Swallow) by
 Giacomo Puccini
Libretto by Giuseppe Adami
Michigan premiere

1972

The Perfect Fool by
 Gustav Holst
Michigan premiere

1975

Mass by Leonard Bernstein
Midwest premiere

1976

Washington Square by
 Thomas Pasatieri
Libretto by Kenward Elmslie
World premiere

1977

Regina by Marc Blitzstein
Libretto by the composer
 from the play by
 Lillian Hellman
Midwest premiere

1978

Singers by Charles Strouse
Commissioned by Michigan
 Opera Theatre
World premiere

1979

The Emperor Jones by
 Louis Gruenberg
Michigan premiere

1980

Of Mice and Men by
 Carlisle Floyd
Michigan premiere

1981

Anoush by Armen Tigranian
Based on a poem by
 Hovhannes Toumanian
English version translated by
 Gerald Papasian
North American premiere

1982

The Haunted Castle (Straszny Dwor)
 by Stanislaw Monuszko
American premiere

Treemonisha by Scott Joplin
Orchestration by Gunther Schuller
Michigan premiere

1984

Sweeney Todd by Stephen Sondheim
Major American opera
 company premiere

1992

King Roger by Karol Szymanowski
Libretto by Jarosław Iwaszkiewicz
American premiere of the original-
 language production

2003

Dead Man Walking by Jake Heggie
Libretto by Terrence McNally
Michigan premiere

2005

Margaret Garner by
    Richard Danielpour
Libretto by Toni Morrison
World premiere

2007

Cyrano by David DiChiera
Libretto by Bernard Uzan
Orchestration by Mark D. Flint
World premiere

2012

Julius Caesar by
    George Frideric Handel
Libretto by Nicola Francesco Haym
Michigan premiere

2014

A View from the Bridge by
    William Bolcom
Libretto by Arnold Weinstein and
    Arthur Miller
Michigan premiere

2015

Frida by Robert Xavier Rodriguez
Book by Hilary Blecher
Lyrics and Monologues by
    Migdalia Cruz
Michigan premiere

The Passenger by
    Mieczyslaw Weinberg
Libretto by Alexander Medvedev
Michigan premiere

2016

Silent Night by Kevin Puts
Libretto by Mark Campbell
Michigan Premiere

Appendix 3   121

Appendix 4: MOT's Community Programs Department Premieres

1975

Vigilance by Karen V. DiChiera
Libretto by Joan Hill

1976

Summer Snow by Fred Rogers

1977

Pete, the Pirate by
 Karen V. DiChiera
Libretto by Joan Hill

1978

Rumpelstiltskin by David and
 Karen V. DiChiera
Libretto by Joan Hill

Look to the Land by
 Karen V. DiChiera
Libretto by Joan Hill

1981

Under One Roof by
 Karen V. DiChiera
Libretto by Joan Hill

1982

Fair Means or Foul by
 Seymour Barab

1985

Musicians of Bremen by Al Balkin

Let's Play Bach by James Eiler

1986

The Night Harry Stopped Smoking by
 Ross Dabrusin and John Davies

1987

Nanabush by Karen V. DiChiera
Libretto by William Kirk

The Frog Who Became a Prince by
 Edward Barnes

1988

Monkey See, Monkey Do by
 Robert Xavier Rodriguez

1989

Ke Nu and the Magic Coals by
 James Hartway
Libretto by Anca Vlasopolos and
 Anthony Ambrogio

The Great Grammar Revue by
 Karen V. DiChiera
Libretto by William Kirk

1990

Cheering Up a Princess by Doug
 Berent and Douglas Braverman

1991

La Pizza Con Fungi by
 Seymour Barab

Let's Play Mozart by Christine Jones

1992

The Tiger of Chungshan by
 Nicholas Scarim

1993

My House Is Too Small by
 Maia Aprahamian

1994

Aesop's Fables by Lawrence Singer
Libretto by Douglas Braverman

1998

Jack and the Beanstalk by
 John Davies
Adapted from Arthur Sullivan

2001

*The Cadillacs and Their Great Lakes
 Adventures* by Karen V. DiChiera
Libretto by Bonnie Lee
 Moss Rattner

2002

The Pied Piper by Seymour Barab

2004

The Araboolies of Liberty Street by
 Ron Perera
Libretto by Constance Congdon

2015

How Nanita Learned to Make Flan
 by Enrique Gonzales-Medina
Libretto by Campbell Geeslin

About the Author

Tim Lentz is currently employed by Michigan Opera Theatre as archivist and director of the Dance and Opera Resource Library at the Detroit Opera House. He also serves on the Advisory Board for the School of Library and Information Science at Wayne State University. He received his B.S. in mechanical engineering at Michigan State University, his secondary certificate in mathematics at Wayne State, and his music credentials at Oakland University. He completed his M.A. and his Ph.D. in theatre and dramatic music literature at Wayne State University. Among other duties, he continues to chronicle the history of the company, and recently his essay "The History of Michigan Opera Theatre," which was included in the David DiChiera 2013 Kresge Eminent Artist monograph, was awarded a first place for feature writing by the Society of Professional Journalists / Detroit Chapter.

In 2006, when the construction on the Broadway Street side of the Detroit Opera House was completed, David DiChiera asked Dr. Lentz to create a library and archive as a permanent resource center. Starting with an empty room, Dr. Lentz created the Allesee Dance and Opera Resource Library / MOT Archive. It is the official library and archive for Michigan Opera Theatre and specializes in materials specific to dance, opera, and MOT's fifty-year history. Dr. Lentz also led the effort to establish a website that makes the library/archive resources available to the public.

At Michigan Opera Theatre, Dr. Lentz is also managing an ongoing project with Wayne State University training library and information science interns. In addition, he managed a major project with Michigan Virtual University, leading a team that developed and designed a fully credited distance-learning course on opera and music theatre titled "The Search for Cyrano," which was available online as of fall 2010 to all Michigan high school students.

Dr. Lentz taught in the Rochester Community Schools for thirty-five years, with thirty-one years as vocal music director / theatre coordinator at Adams High School. He was selected as a state finalist for the 1982 Michigan Teacher of the Year and has been listed in Who's Who among America's Teachers seven times. Dr. Lentz received a Certificate of Appreciation from the National Honor Roll, was nominated for 2006–2007 Michigan Teacher of the Year, and was awarded Rochester Community School's Excellence in Education Award in 2003. He was very active in the Michigan School Vocal Music Association (MSVMA) and served on MSVMA's Executive Board as treasurer for eighteen years. He also has an extensive theatre résumé, including directing productions at Wayne State and freelance work directing in Detroit area dinner theatres, as well as directing over one hundred productions for the Rochester Community Schools.